Prisons with Stained Glass Windows

jonathan r walton

Copyright © 2014 jonathan r walton

All rights reserved.

ISBN-13:978-0-9794055-7-0

DEDICATION

This book is dedicated to every lost and hurting person around the globe. I hope and pray that the words on this page and the passion with which I have undertaken this writing will touch the hearts of all who read it. I pray that God's anointing would birth a fire in every reader to consume their world with the power of apostolic anointing. I pray that your lives will never be the same, and that you will soon be reached by someone who carries the wonderful message of Jesus Christ.

CONTENTS

	Forward: By Aaron Holloway	1
	Introduction	2
1	Is Evangelism Killing Revival?	8
2	A Thin Red Line	34
3	The Key and the Door	58
4	Love is the Movement	84
5	The Devil is in the Details	98
6	The Marketplace	120
7	Absolutes of Convenience	140
8	The Church's Response to the Family Paradigm Shift	154
9	Problems, Passion, and Purpose	178
10	Prisons With Stained Glass Windows	212
	Conclusion	236

ACKNOWLEDGMENTS

I would like to acknowledge my great friend, Aaron Holloway. Our many discussions on trying to reach people in this hour has kept me motivated. I hope this book captures the essence of what we have prayed about and discussed. You are a great leader and spiritual young man who is passionate about God and His Kingdom, and you have not yet started to see what God is going to do through your ministry.

I would also like to thank the many people who have influenced my life concerning soul winning. My pastor and father-in-law, Rick Pavlu, who has built a wonderful church in Church Point, Louisiana, that I am honored to be part of. Church Point is a little town in the middle of nowhere, but it has a thriving, powerful church that is hungry for revival. Thank my good friend, Andrew Handy, who never misses an opportunity to tell someone about Jesus. Our Bible study coordinator at The Church Point Pentecostals, Clint Credeur, whose compassion for others always runs deep. And I would be remiss to not mention G.A., Vesta, and Anthony Mangun. I have never had the privilege to speak with any of these great heroes personally. However, I cannot remember hearing a message by any one of them that did not put me on my face before God with a deep hunger to reach the world around me. Those messages helped shaped the heart of a young man deciding to do something for God.

Lastly. A very special thank you to all the people who don't leave your Christianity in the foyer of the church when you exit the building. Thank you for living the purpose of the Kingdom in your everyday life. Only eternity will reveal the magnitude of what you precious people have accomplished in the Name of Jesus.

FOREWORD
By: Aaron Holloway

I have the utmost confidence and respect for this author. His insight and God given revelation of the word for this book are truly enlightening.

2 Kings 6:1-7 tells about some men who had outgrown their dwelling. They set out to build a bigger one. Their motives were pure, for they wanted to build a bigger place to further the work of God. You cannot fault their work ethic. They had a plan, but the tool needed most to complete the task was soon lost. They lost the axe head.

I feel this church age has the right motives, work ethic, and programs. We even have vision. However, the tools needed most in this hour seem to be missing. No amount of "good" programs will ever trump a consecrated prayer life that produces apostolic anointing. We can strike a tree all day long with an axe handle. It might even feel right because it's for a good cause. However, we will only wear ourselves out with nothing to show but a tree with scarred bark.

This book will arrest multiple generations' attention and place at their disposal the original tools of winning souls and having revival. Jonathan Walton shows us that the missing axe head is still exactly where we left it.

INTRODUCTION

The promise for prominence of Pentecostal power, authority, and anointing accompanying the apostle's lifestyle and doctrine is rapidly becoming a reality. However, despite this promise, many Christians remain gridlocked in the grind of mere existence, forever facing a frustrating illusion of mediocrity. Depression, anxiety, stress, and sickness are far too common in the church. For many, the idea of living in the victory of Christ and the early apostles is a distant dream rapidly fading into oblivion. The potential for anointing is evident. The Biblical assurance of end-time revival is unmistakable. Why then do many live beneath the possibilities of the Kingdom?

At the root of this dilemma is the way in which we view ourselves. Society and modern philosophy have stolen the highly progressive nature that was the hallmark of apostolic men and women in the New Testament. They lived under Kingdom principles that have lost value in current culture. The church teeters on a ledge of confusion, speaking out of both sides of our mouth. On one hand, we assert that the enemy is causing more destruction, fighting harder, and attacking more ferociously than ever. We allege that Satan knows his time is short and is launching a desperate offensive to destroy the church. As a result, we must ward off the influx of evil attempting to sneak into our midst, battle Satan's malicious attempts to undermine the family, and protect new converts and young people more than ever before.

However, if we are not careful, we allow the enemy to deceive us into a state of complacency whereby we attempt to wage the greatest war the church has ever known with less than it has ever possessed. We pursue more power but practice less prayer. We strive for more authority while displaying less submission. We prepare for more depth and growth but with weaker faith. We desire a supernatural culture but desire less church. Times are different, people are busy, and the economy is tough. In accommodating others and making life more convenient for ourselves, is it possible that we could plan God right out of our midst? Is it possible to be more spiritually aware but with less spiritual focus?

The early church didn't face the same economic hardships, partly because they had shared everything to make sure that all people were cared for. Despite the fact they didn't have the same economic burdens or busy schedules, they did contend with a culture that killed and tortured people for worshipping God or spreading His gospel. Modern inconveniences faced in the American church are nothing compared to the "difficulties" of the early hardships. However, the enemy's plan is to make Christianity less committed and less dependant on God's principles, while steadfastly arguing that we need more commitment and dependency. Is it possible that we could become too blessed to be apostolic?

Ironically, the most constant semblance the modern

church has to consistent apostolic ministry is found overseas in third world countries. They are witnessing great numbers being filled with the Holy Ghost. They see more consistent and higher numbers of miracles, signs, and wonders. It is paradoxical, because if the belief system of the American church is accurate, the opposite should be taking place. The churches with the easiest schedules and least opposition should be growing most. However, the places void of religious freedom experience more spiritual deliverance. This suggests that outward oppression cannot stop apostolic revival. Apostolic anointing can and will only be stopped from within.

The danger of this hour is that the enemy is not concerned that we give ourselves to the church. He does not want us to give ourselves to God. Under his plan, we learn religion and call it relationship. We learn to give and label it sacrifice. We keep a few responsibilities and call it commitment. We do those few responsibilities well and label it excellence. We learn to win a few souls and pass it off as revival. We learn to sing a few songs and call it worship. We learn to say a few words and say we've prayed. We step out when God has clearly spoken only after studying every aspect of what He instructed, and we call that faith. We follow a few rules and pretend it is obedience. We aspire to look a certain way and call it holiness. We present a few details of our lives and call it submission. We reach for only our own families and friends and call it love. This is the danger of being lulled to sleep in the comfortable American church.

The cross is not decayed. The blood is not diluted by watered down religious concepts portrayed as apostolic truth.

The challenges and controversies of young, contemporary dreamers have not paralyzed the brazenness and clarity of God's Word. The empty tomb is not just a distantly remembered landmark. The bloody stripes and dangling flesh of the Master have not been reduced to mere images of a mega film. Healing, deliverance, power, authority, anointing, and salvation are still alive in the bosom of the church.

Central to this apostolic outpouring is God's love for lost people. Every detail from creation to Calvary revolves around the thematic imagery of fallen humanity returning to intimacy with God. Previous generations have established a solid foundation of holiness and doctrinal theology. The focus of many mainline churches has been on the inner circle, strengthening the core, preparing the framework for a great outpouring of God's Spirit in the last days. Currently, leaders have realized that the outpouring is here. They are launching into the progressive realm of possibility that Scripture details. The shift of current mainstream methodology has moved from internal strengthening to external gathering. Reaching the world by any means possible has become the hallmark cry of this generation. However, in any great transition there is enormous vulnerability. This is not a moment to ignorantly ignore details or defiantly defend beliefs. It's a season to examine reality and face the Truth. What does God say about the pivotal issues?

Spreading the gospel of the risen Savior is the main priority of the church. Making Jesus famous among the world is our job description. It has always been God's official mandate. New Testament theology validates the notion that the apostolic church needs to influence the world. One cannot truly measure the value of a soul. Many reputable leaders have recognized that the church needs to do a better job of marketing and influencing the lost on terms and by means that the world can understand. However, modern views concerning evangelism are so strong that they have replaced the need for revival in many churches. We recognize that this is a subtle snare of the enemy, and we must avoid this mentality at all cost.

> **We cannot use the apostolic agenda as an excuse to deviate from apostolic nature.**

Evangelism is horizontal, a reaching for lost people. Revival is vertical, a passionate move toward God. The two terms have almost meshed. If new people are coming to church, we consider that to be a move of God and a sign that we are in God's perfect will. Current church culture is so fascinated with evangelism that it has forgotten that the true power of reaching people comes only through our connection to God. Long-term success will never come through producing culturally relevant programs alone. We must not lose intimacy with the Father because of principles that supposedly prioritize God's agenda, but in reality, if made the solitary focus, only weaken it.

Under current terminology, evangelism is possible without revival. However, God's Word reveals the opposite. Revival always produces growth. People's lives will be positively impacted when a group of people truly pursue God. The lost are reached whenever the church plans toward a God-focus. We must find the balance between the evangelism and revival. We must not lose God in attempts to reach men for Him. He must remain our ultimate objective. A church that reaches people outside of apostolic authority and anointing is only establishing positive numeric trends. A church reaching people in apostolic authority and anointing is building people and changing lives. We cannot use the apostolic agenda as an excuse to deviate from our apostolic nature. The enemy wants nothing more than for us to confuse building "a" church with our call to build "the" church. We must forever look toward Jesus, keeping Him the center of everything that we do. Our church logo must not supercede the fame of His name. Our mission statements must not be more memorable than His Holy Word. Our planning to reach the world on a natural level in necessary, but it must not become more important than our practice of reaching God.

1
IS EVANGELISM KILLING REVIVAL?

Core values define any entity. A company makes its name by what it invests in. Mission statements clearly indicate priorities. Hidden within the nucleus of these avowals is the commercial agenda, the mainstay focus of the corporation. Staying true to this center is what propels most into prominence. Failure to fixate on these principles causes fatal fluctuations in overall aptitude.

The church's agenda has never been more muddled. Christ clearly communicated the schema to His carefully chosen disciples. The first step is to love the Lord with all thy heart, soul, mind, and strength. The mandate is to serve, seek, please, and live for Him. This principle was reiterated when Christ taught the disciple's that they were to seek God's

Kingdom above all else. Later, Jesus instructed them to wait for the power of the Holy Ghost before preaching the gospel to the world.

The enemy wants our modern methods of evangelism to subvert this order. Our adversary plans to make our mantra (Reach the world at all costs) undermine God's first commandment. We must remember that before God earmarked that we are to love others as ourselves and sacrifice for those we don't even know, He demanded connectivity and intimacy toward Him.

> **In choosing to expand outward, we must not forget that our first priority is upward.**

Contemporary Christianity has shifted outward. The wise have cried for the church to move beyond its walls, and the church has responded swiftly and passionately. However, the danger has been that in choosing to expand outward, we've forgotten that our first priority is upward.

Seeking God and His righteousness first is still the key to natural success. However, this success most often requires patience, because God is into developing people for future purpose, adding value to every life, not just becoming a quick fix for failure. Therefore, when lacking spiritual fortitude, it's easy to trust gimmicks and programs more than Christ to build feelings of accomplishment.

Success presents a problem because it must be defined. Numbers become the measuring stick by which we compare ourselves. Many Christians blindly do whatever it takes to press forward in statistical trends. We have forgotten that no met goal is a success unless God has defined the goal, and no unmet goal is a failure unless God has labeled as such. The pursuit of numerical perfection must not steal the authenticity that only comes through yielding wholly to God.

Measurements are dangerous to faith. Calculations are detrimental to the hopes of those following Christ. Most importantly, they are contrary to the development and demonstration of true love. The author of Corinthians wrote that love does not keep score. True love is not present where someone's wrongs are constantly used against them. It also disclosed that true love is not present where the motive for "loving" is empirically driven. However, many sinners find themselves sought after as part of a numbers crunch. One devalues God's purpose if the motives for reaching outward are not as simple as seeking and saving the lost because that is what God desires. We must proceed vigilantly, for the enemy is the master deceiver. He is great at convincing God's people to unknowingly do the right thing for the wrong reasons.

PREJUDICE STILL EXISTS

Many churches reach poor communities to spread the gospel of Christ. This is admirable. However, it leads to an issue not widely discussed in many religious circles. Most people shy away from the topics of prejudice and racism. In a church supposedly built on love, how is it conceivable that prejudice exists? Most scoff at the notion that the church could be prejudiced or biased against any culture or color.

However, just because racism or prejudice is no longer overt does not mean it no longer exists.

The problem with discussions such as racism and prejudice is that most people only consider the extremes. They feel that because no one is calling clandestine meetings where church members wear white sheets and burn crosses, God's love must have permeated to the core and utterly eradicated all forms of racism and prejudice from the church. However, although these issues are not as overt in mainstream Christianity, they are still present and should not be ignored.

The Word of God dictates that any church refusing to become multicultural because of fear, intimidation, or tradition is not of God. The doors to the church are never closed to anyone… Ever… Period.

Nothing is more against God's nature than for a church to proclaim to be established on His Word, but still refuse to allow certain people to enter their building based on preconceived ideas. At times, it's may not be disallowed, but neither is it encouraged, and that's just as wrong.

However, the dilemma is that this isn't the only way prejudice and racism can be demonstrated by the church. The enemy seldom destroys through observable assaults. He's much more subtle and silent. Like a cancer that must be totally eradicated, he looks to infiltrate core values of God's people. The life of the church has been and will forever remain unprecedented, unrestrained, and unbiased love.

Most Christians believe they possess Christ-like love

because they build on religious principles. Attach a few moral codes to live by, throw in a few distinguishing doctrinal details, add a greater spiritual focus to daily living, season it with decisions toward self-sacrifice, and suddenly one has the perfect storm toward self-destruction.

> **The greatest deception of all is self-deception.**

That may sound absurd to some. However, self-deception is the greatest deception of all. The tide of self-sufficiency silently overwhelms many Christians. This attitude says, "I appear holy, do well, and think wholesome thoughts; therefore, I'm a devoted servant of God." However, that statement is not always true. One may be kind to people of another race, but that does not prove they have no prejudiced or racist views. This will probably open the proverbial can of worms, but it's an issue the church should not ignore.

> **Jesus left His mark on a life without leaving His brand name.**

Jesus dealt with this issue on a consistent basis. He touched lepers, dealt with the poor, and talked with those of questionable character. He befriended prostitutes, even allowing one to wash his holy feet with her soiled and bitter tears. He allowed foreigners access to blessings that were not theologically or dispensationally available. He defied Jewish tradition in order to bless people who could give nothing back. He demonstrated the actions that He wanted His church to later duplicate.

So what is the problem? It is true that most innovative churches already do this things. We have ministries designed to blend into the underprivileged parts of society. So what is the point? The point is that Jesus did this and expected nothing in return. He did not do it to grow a church. He did not walk among the paupers and peasants for natural gain. He left them as quietly as He had entered, always leaving them better than when He'd came. Jesus left His mark on a life without leaving His brand name. He didn't need recognition, deferring all glory to the Father. To Jesus, it was about touching, blessing, helping, and ultimately changing others.

Imagine this scenario unfolding. Jesus walks up to His disciples after a long day. The dreadful dust of the dirty Samaritan desert still clings to His garments and soils His sandals.

"Hello boys, guess what I did today? I went down to the well for a while. The lowly, Samaritan women go there to draw water. I knew I could talk to some of them. You know, they are poor and needy. Finally, one came who desperately needed a change. I spoke with her a while, giving revelation and insight into eternal life. What a day. I feel virtuous now."

Some of the disciples stand in disbelief. How could this vast and noble Jesus go into places like that? He had dirtied himself where most dignitaries wouldn't be seen. However, a couple of the disciples grew excited by His story,

"You did it again, Jesus," John states, "It makes us feel so good when you do something like this."

Peter follows John by patting Jesus on the back, "You sure did something awesome today. It's wonderful to know you touched someone that most of the world doesn't even notice."

Jesus stands back a little and looks at Peter, "Why Pete, it does feel good. I got my hands dirty again. Dealing with people who aren't as intelligent, gifted, blessed, and spiritual as us is surely the work of the Father. I cannot wait to get back to the synagogue and share our exploits with the others. We should go next weekend too. We could probably bring food for those unfortunate souls. Perhaps a few would come to church. Then, we could justify our expenses for the food and drinks. If we told the pastor, I bet he'd be excited. Ah, life is good."

Does that not devalue what took place at the well? Yes, a woman's life was temporarily impacted in that version of the story. However, Jesus' attitude indicates that although the actions were unquestionably genuine, the motives were ridiculously selfish?

In reality, Jesus never acted that way. He was there because He sincerely loved people. There were no ulterior motives or hidden agendas. He wasn't merely reacting to a church growth strategy. He was there to meet needs because He actually cared. It was that simple.

Whenever Jesus encountered people who had spiritual and natural needs, He took care of both. It didn't matter if the ends justified the means. He wasn't around long enough to see if His meritorious deeds paid off by financial or numerical increase. When it came to helping hurting people, compassion moved Jesus to the point that He stopped caring about the religious. He was too in love with the lost individual to worry about potential cost. This was the very attribute that would lead Him to Calvary to pay the price for all of humanity.

Most have heard, "If we reach those that no one wants, God will give us those that everyone wants." This statement is extremely true. However, it carries an enormous philosophical problem. The issue is not with the philosophy itself, for the theory is proven. If people demonstrate the love of God, the church will grow.

The problem is not with the people who started these type of campaigns that are rapidly gaining popularity across the country. The latest proponents of these techniques have a track record that speaks for itself. I am in no way undermining or criticizing their work. What they do for the Kingdom of God is truly amazing.

The problem with this methodology is that someone had to create a motive to get the North American church involved in the communities with the greatest needs. The concern is that those with a passion to reach the lost, help hurting people, spread the love of Christ, give hope to the helpless, and bring joy into sadness, actually had to create a reason for the body of Christ to engage in God's original purpose. Where is Christ's love in that?

Several impressive churches, led by prominent men reach into underprivileged communities for the right reasons. Every time Pastor Anthony Mangun, from The Pentecostals of Alexandria, discusses evangelism, one can literally feel the passion of a man on fire to serve God's purpose in the world. It energizes the room when such men enthusiastically speak from a heart of true compassion for the lost. Their churches grow because they've found a way to engage culture without compromising apostolic power.

The enemy does not care if you reach into what he considers his territory, if you do so with polluted motives. That is why the church needs an awareness of its reasons for reaching outward. Only genuine self-examination will reveal truth. Do I feel distinguished or better about myself when I've gone into underprivileged places? Do I discuss it with others as if to pin medals on my chest? Do I talk down to people while I'm there, even if unintended? Do I truly view them as equal to me, or am I pretentiously elevating myself? Do I try to help whether I ever see them again, or am I only serving them because I expect them to attend my church? If there are twenty new people the following service is it worth it, whereas if no one shows up, it is unsuccessful?

I am not advocating that we should not want new people in our churches. I'm not even stating that we shouldn't try to use these methods to connect with people. What I am suggesting is that success for such events should not be defined by how many come to church each time I give something. Success should not be measured by how much the people I have invested in reciprocate back to me. True success must still be measures in eternity, and that is something we do not have the privilege of knowing. Our job is to serve and try to connect. God's job is to give the increase.

If we were brutally honest, many of us would discover questionable motives in our outreach efforts. We would discover that we feel "proud" for what we've accomplished.

If no preconceived feelings of superiority exist, then why do these experiences result in self-exaltation? Why do I view myself as having accomplished something significant? Why, if I talk about God to people who are just like me, does it feel vastly different from when I go into these "less fortunate" places?

God has placed infinite value on every soul. The motive is to save, help, and touch every person. When evangelizing like Jesus, one must forget the bottom line expectations of church growth and identify the value of each person being encountered. That concept seems so foreign when the main focus is numerical increase. However, the way to expand the Kingdom has never been to focus on the growth. The way to build the Kingdom has been twofold. Focus on God and focus on others. We must recognize the absolute importance of connecting every person to Christ so that they can discover the absolute value they possess through Him. If numerical growth is the only goal, we will most often fail. However, if spiritual growth and impacting lives for Christ is the goal, we will succeed, and numerical growth will occur.

CIRCUMSTANTIAL COMPASSION

The rain beats mercilessly upon the hard-packed earth. One man stands behind the rest, yelling a cadence at the top of his lungs. With each word, fog escapes his mouth, a visible indication of the frigidity in the air.

However, the cold atmosphere has done nothing to quiet the crowd. They revel in the moment. The home team has the ball at the three-yard line.

Down by four points.

Two seconds left on the clock.

It is playoff football... Win or go home.

The quarterback lifts his arms up and down, asking the crowd to quiet down so his players can hear his calls. The once screaming crowd has grown silent. The quarterback examines the defense, knowing the play clock is getting low.

Seven, six, five...

He is not nervous. This is why he studied all those hours. It's why he has watched days of video footage on the opposition. He was the first one in the weight room and the last one off the practice field. He spent extra time in the coach's office because of this innate drive to win.

He lifts his right leg, sending the halfback in motion. Suddenly, he notices something. It was only a flinch, but it was there. The strong safety inched forward. Maybe it was only his eyes, perhaps a shift in his feet. Whatever it was, the quarterback instinctively knew that the safety was about to blitz.

To most quarterbacks, that would mean pressure off the left side, but not to him. To him, it meant there would be no safety help on that half of the field.

The quarterback quickly barked a hot read to the receiver. Then, one more time, he looked at the defense. He was almost smiling as the ball hit his fingers. This was a crucial moment, but it was routine. He and the wide receiver had practices this hundreds of times in practice.

The receiver timed it perfect, breaking off his post route and darting to the back of the end zone on a fade. The cornerback was confused, as the ball sailed over his head.

"Touchdown... Touchdown... Touchdown," the announcer yelled over the intercom.

The receiver spiked the ball into the dampened dirt, splashing water two feet into the air. He then broke into a wild dance. The crowd was frenzied, yelling as loud as they could. Partiers spilled their drinks, strangers high-fived, and grown men hugged in the rapture of this moment.

The players on the field formed a pile on the receiver. Screaming. Tears of relief and joy. This was the moment they'd fought for. They were the champions.

This is a classic moment in the life of an American athlete who has won a championship. Most Americans consider these actions acceptable under the circumstances. My purpose isn't to discuss whether those antics are appropriate or wrong, but rather to prove a point.

If the circumstances were different, if there were ten minutes left in the first quarter, if the team had been going for a first down instead of a touchdown, the reaction to the same play would've been different. Some players make routine plays at low-pressure moments, but still make a sizeable show of it. They come across as immature, for they think they've accomplished something noteworthy. If it's not significant, then don't pretend it is. One's reaction should always indicate the intensity of the moment. An overreaction usually indicates misguided motives, which most often leads to over promotion of self.

Jesus was constantly moved into action by the multitudes that thronged Him. He stopped and paid attention to individuals He met. A short tax collector in a tree, an outcast at a well, a prostitute in a rich man's house, a desperate father, a grieving mother; Jesus stopped for them, and He did so without demonstrating a sense of overwhelming accomplishment. He did His duty, and He did not embellish it later.

The overwhelming sense of accomplishment that has often been demonstrated by those "working for the Kingdom of God" is interesting. Some will not involve themselves in a "significant" work unless there is recognition to be gained. On one hand, they criticize the disadvantaged for being needy, claiming that in this country, with all the opportunity available, everyone has a chance to be successful. Compassion toward the hurting is missing. Deeper feelings are often ignored. Some saints privately voice negative feelings toward the poor only to publicly become their advocates.

This may fool many people in the church who are eager to help. However, God notices self-promoting attitudes. Ironically, so do people who are used to surviving on the streets. They are used to being played by everyone around them. They've learned to recognize genuine love when they see it. People know who truly cares and who is just blowing hot air. They are not as easily manipulated as it may seem, and the main concern is once a church gets the reputation of only pursuing numbers, no one wants to attend. People despise churches that do not truly care about them on an individual level. No one wants to be part of a number's crunch.

NOT BY CHOICE

There is a common misconception that most people are the way they are solely by choice. This is a highly biased viewpoint and does nothing to further the love that Christ demonstrated. It's extremely narrow minded of most white, middle-class Christians to feel that their interpretation of life is the only one that makes sense. A white American from a middle-class subdivision has an extremely different mindset than an African-American from an impoverished ghetto.

I'm going to compare these two lifestyles, not because this is the only time bigotry occurs, but to shed insight into how easy it is to allow feelings we shouldn't possess to supersede reasonable judgment. Preconceived ideas keep believers from presenting God as He desires to be seen.

White, middle-class Christians often reach into black deprived neighborhoods with the same feelings in which most people visit nursing homes. They do not view the people through common lenses of equality. They view them from a lofty plain that suggests these people are broken, marred, and in desperate need of repair because of the way they live, not because they need Jesus.

Judging from the precepts and constructs of a white, middle-class upbringing, this seems true. However, on the street, the rules are different. Everything is not the way it appears. The young, African-American drug dealer on the corner doesn't think he's broken or out of sync with society. He's living the only way he knows how. He's surviving by the methods that have been modeled to him, just as the white, middle-class person is.

One cannot bring a supremacist attitude into the street culture ruled by street cred (respect) and expect to be accepted. The people there aren't interested in being fixed. They're just like every white, American man. They do not want to be disrespected in front of those they know, especially by someone they don't know.

I've heard white women state about poor African-American women raising their children, "They don't love their kids much to let them run the streets like that."

That observation is far from reality. Suggest that to the face of one of those mothers, and in most cases the result would be disastrous. Such statements profoundly demonstrate the ignorance with which many try to reach people of different cultures. We try to convert different cultures; not only to doctrine, but also to our way of life, and often, this is the very reason our doctrine is rejected. We must force God's Word to be ignored because we are too busy advancing our way of living.

The truth is that white, middleclass America lives the way it does because that's what society has taught and demonstrated. It is the social norm. White suburbia has its own social codes to live by.

Guess what? The Ghetto has its own rules as well. What white suburbia frowns upon, the other side routinely lives. The point is that many from posh, safe environments have a tremendously hard time feeling compassion toward those from the slums who seem to exhibit no desire to better their lives.

This also works the opposite way. I have a great friend that I spent hours with studying through graduate school. She is an exceptionally gifted, highly intelligent, African-American girl that has turned into a highly successful healthcare professional. She once shared how hard it was to go home from college and talk with the people she used to hang around. Many of them didn't go to college, and instead of applauding her accomplishments, they ridiculed her for "trying to be white." It offended her that they were so closed minded to feel that an African-American who chose to pursue a higher education was somehow degrading her own culture. The point is that both sides of this argument make the same mistake, viewing the world only through their own limited constructs.

On a kingdom level, this mistake presents major outreach problems and is one reason that modern evangelism strangles what made the apostolic church powerful. Jesus continually dealt with multicultural issues, and He always met people on their terms. He never compromised Truth, but He never disrespected a person because of their environmental constructs. After gaining trust and demonstrating respect, Jesus brought them into the arena of Truth. His success was based on performance more than position or programs.

The early apostolic church dealt with culturally charged

controversies as well. Some men dealt arrogantly with others on the terms of what they knew. However, as the gospel began to spread, they learned that the most effective way into the heart of others is to present the gospel with equal parts love and respect, not from pity.

Most often, people live the way they do because it's what society has taught them. If there is to be hope to turn an adolescent from the life of crime and drugs common in his environment, the way is not to point out the dangers and moral wrongs of that environment. One must first take that child in with loving arms, committing to a process that's years in the making, treating that child as one of your own, giving, helping, encouraging, protecting, advocating, and promoting with passion. Over time, the love of God will take root, and a higher purpose will be revealed. When man allows God to govern, it always works, because God transcends culture. Then, the change is not equated to a cultural one but an eternal one.

If a drug dealer or habitual user is to be reached, it will be when those in the church quit viewing him differently and start loving him as equal through the blood of Christ. The church will only be effective at reaching other cultures when it ignores differences and focuses on what others can become through God. When a single, unemployed mother of four, surviving off of welfare is treated just as hospitably as the doctors' wife, the church will reach her. Is it wrong for her to live the life she is? To most in the church, the answer would be yes. However, that life is all she knows. It is who she is, because it's all she has seen, and she will not change because those in the middle-class tell her she should. However, she will make changes according to the revelation of true love that comes when her spirit is affected by the power of God's Spirit. Through love and true acceptance, she cannot remain the same. That is true Christianity.

There's far too much judgment in the church, even when we don't realize we're guilty of it. To reach those that are different, the church must first learn to accept the differences. Not approve of them but at least accept them. And the acceptance cannot be from a motive to change a person's lifestyle. It must be demonstrated solely because that is what true love does. It finds the good in everyone and loves unconditionally. If one has not walked in the shoes of those from the other side of the tracks, then there is no room for judgment. True love and respect break cultural barriers and set others free.

A GOOD CHRISTIAN OR A GOOD PERSON?

The modern evangelical system has created an excellent opportunity for those looking to gain popularity and advantage within the church. The works by which men were "measured" (and I use that term extremely loosely) in the Bible days was not of manmade description. Paul acknowledged that he still felt like a sinner even after becoming a prolific apostle. He never felt like he was above others. He didn't use eloquent words to sound educated. Instead, he came with the demonstration of the Spirit.

The measuring stick of Christianity was once the intimate working of the Holy Ghost. If men could draw crowds, preach stirring messages, shake a thousand hands, or entice an entire multitude, it didn't matter. Numbers didn't define the early church. They weren't into the numbers game.

Immediately many would argue based on scriptures in the New Testament that highlight that "many were added to the church daily," or "that same day were added about three thousand souls." However, the reason for the numbers in these texts wasn't to highlight the growth alone. On the contrary, the significance was in highlighting the power of God's Spirit. The outpouring was so clear and effective that many were added to the church as a result. They weren't focused on the numbers. They were focused on the spirit, and because of this original focus, the church grew exponentially.

> A redistribution of balance within the church rarely shakes out evenly.

The early church did not focus on empirical data in their teachings. Instead, they focused on concepts of prayer, fasting, worship, commitment, discipleship, love, kindness, faith, preaching, holiness, and apostolic anointing that breaks changes, delivers the oppressed, heals the sick, and saves the lost. They grew in number because they were empowered with God's presence. The early church was not powerful because it had numbers. Rather, it had numbers because it was powerful.

To the early church leadership, if the eternal impact was unusually small, the leadership wasn't concerned. They understood that charisma without power brings change that will not last. That's why Paul mentioned possessing a nature that brought miracles, signs, and wonders. They were committed to bringing more than natural works.

Today, we try to maintain balance between the natural and spiritual worlds. However, we cannot be so spiritually minded that we're of no earthly value. We must not only strive to make people feel awkward or uncomfortable around us. We cannot only meet a person's spiritual needs. We must meet natural needs as well. Knowing this, we create new constructs that extend more into the natural realm. These new rules are acceptable and were created by wise men. However, the problem with this philosophy is that it creates a redistribution of balance that rarely shakes out evenly. Any time a new direction is given, most of the focus is on ensuring that the church meets that new directive. Therefore, the new system is highly unstable. We've tried so desperately to create balance that if not careful, we shift the focus in the opposite direction.

If not careful, the enemy uses this to deceptively establish a system in which it's easier for good people to thrive than it is for good Christians. There's a vast difference between the two. Understanding this difference will probably save many from ultimately falling to this deception. It's easy, under current philosophical systems, to believe that one is in right standing with God based solely on performance. The belief is that if I'm doing charitable deeds, I'm doing the work of a Christian. Therefore, I am a Christian.

There's an obvious problem with this mentality. Ever meet a congenial Muslim? A kind-hearted atheist? A hardworking Buddhist? A world changer of unchristian origin? A popular Scientologist? Of course, if one has attempted to share Christ's love in this multicultural world, he has witnessed positive change from many sources. If not, just read the news. It is full of people making a difference in times of significant crisis and natural disaster. Athletes and movie stars pour millions into charities every year. All of them are good Christians based on their sizable charitable contributions, right?

Many Christians scoff at that idea. Many of these Hollywood stars are professing atheist. Many give to gain positive publicity or promote their next film. The point is that believers discredit others' "Christian" works because they don't live "Christian" lifestyles. We challenge their motives, recognizing that it's entirely possible to do 'good' works without being a devoted follower of God.

However, in the church, we often follow the same routines without evaluating motives. We feel that because we attend church and have Christ centered theology, good works somehow prove our level of Christianity. This is far from the Truth.

If someone within the church does a "good" deed we believe it's Christian works. However, if someone outside of the church does the same deed, it's not a Christian work. This cannot be. Obviously, the criterion defining Christian works must be greater than performance of a selfless act. There's a far nobler concept. There are many admirable works in the church that are not necessarily from God.

We judge others by what they're doing. However, as Christians, we shouldn't evaluate the same way as the world. Works cannot save us. That is Biblically evident. Therefore, we should judge ourselves by what we are not doing more than by what we are doing. What spiritual fruit is being produced?

Where is gentleness? It's not found in being sympathetic. Where is true kindness? It's not found in being kind. Where is true love? It's not obtained by demonstrating acts of love. Where is peace? It's not acquired by breaking up fights. All of these are essential qualities, but if there's no established intimacy with God, all the actions being exhibited only make one a good person, regardless of how much one attends church.

It's impossible for one to be an exemplary Christian void of a deep intimacy with Christ. The enemy destroys many people because of a massive misunderstanding on the part of evangelical theology. We've gotten it wrong.

Do well.

Love.

Laugh.

Live.

Eat.

Pray.

Demonstrate kindness.

Work hard.

These modern mantras have made it easy for the non-Christian to thrive in a Christian environment. It is possible for someone with little Godly connection to climb the leadership ranks of the church. Positive leadership qualities, charisma, and effort often outrank anointing. Quick results outweigh the absolute effectiveness of the patient and powerful approach that God often brings through His most anointed vessels. God has never been interested in natural success first. He chose David over seven more appealing brothers. Seven is the number of perfection. Yet, God moved past natural perfection and chose a worshipper with a desire for nothing other than relationship with his Creator.

God chose a stutter-er over an intellect. He chose a rejected dreamer over elder brothers of better report. He chose a lowly virgin and a meek carpenter to bring Christ to the world. He chose a hot-head named Peter and not a more refined doctor or lawyer to preach the first message of His church. He chose a Christian killer to pen half of the New Testament, because He is not into evaluating from a natural perspective.

This misconception may cause many to be lost, for one can be disenfranchised and still "feel" connected. God, in His infinite mercy, continues to allow sinners to feel His presence. Sensitivity to God is never a measure of right standing. Many people disillusion themselves into believing they are still saved because the Almighty moves upon their emotions.

That's why Jesus warned that many believers would use their works as leverage but still be lost. One is not a good Christian because he does good deeds under the guise of religion. The difference is that I cannot make myself a good Christian; only God's transforming power can do that.

Without His transforming power, the most I can do it to become a good person. The main difference between a good person and a good Christian is that a good Christian doesn't live merely from choice but from a nature change. Good Christians are new creatures that have been influenced and changed by God's mercy and grace. Their behavior is different, not by choice, but because God has altered their way of thinking. There are a lot of good people on church pews. God wants good Christians.

I WOULD RATHER REACH ONE

It's easy for the world to prey on true Christians. In a world waiting for handouts, this has never been more evident. The current evangelical trend of using gifts to entice people is increasing. In this culture, most want something for nothing. Society has programmed man to desire as much as possible while giving little. This is the new American way.

Most Christians have a problem with this philosophy when the costs of manpower and monetary expenditures fail to match numerical and financial expectations. The programs are stopped or reallocated if quick progress is not achieved. This leads to a lack of consistency in the church's message toward the underprivileged. The message the impoverished receive is that we are merely offering another program they can't trust. The Federal Government has more credibility.

In this environment, it's difficult for many Christians to not feel like they're being taken advantage of when handing out food in some neighborhoods. Unfortunately, there are a few misguided individuals that jump at the chance to get a handout when it's available. They are only interested in taking.

Many Christian's response is to turn away from these people completely. At times, this is the worst move we could make. People want to know we care about them in their environments before they'll embrace ours. The discomfort they feel coming to our services will only be alleviated when they are convinced that they are unconditionally loved.

What if we viewed each person like Jesus did? We tend to view people as a whole; while Jesus recognized that natural needs are usually indicators of hidden spiritual needs. We must not be afraid to give because a people will abuse our kindness. We cannot miss an open door out of a fear of being taken advantage of. The greater crime is to ignore a need, not show love, not spread joy and hope, and not share Christ. It is worth the risk to reach one person for God.

CONCLUSION

Modern evangelism may be slowly smothering the fires of revival. Revival at its core has always been about connecting man with God. Modern evangelistic trends attempt to connect man to man on the basis of charisma, emotional preaching, gifts, and entertainment. This connection is weak and rarely lasts. As quickly as the fire erupts, it usually burns out.

The world is in dire need of a church that returns to

apostolic power and authority. The church of Acts fixated on the centrality of God and His Word. The apostles didn't venture outside of that. They recognized that the Spirit was in control, and they had no authority outside of it.

If not careful, methods of modern evangelism may jeopardize the flow of the Spirit. There are seasons of harvest and seasons of sowing. If the church only gears for the harvest, it will fail. There must be a season of prayer, fasting, faith development, and work that lays the foundation for revival.

God, help us recognize and follow You above all else. Help us connect and commit to You more than to our church. Help us not have a "works" mentality, but to be changed by your passion for the lost. Help us grow in You first, understanding that You will increase the church when you are glorified. In Jesus Name, amen.

2
A THIN RED LINE

As she staggered into the inner sanctum, her desperation turned to panic. Tears streaked her dust-filled face. Her tousled hair showed the effects of little care. She was not normally so deficient in her appearance. She'd been told that she was an attractive woman. However, if those who had told her that could only see her today, they would change their minds. Unrecognizable, that's how she felt. Her clothes were tarnished and wrinkled. Her eyes were ablaze with a buried fury that she fought to conceal everyday.

The others wouldn't understand. They never had. She'd always been different than her peers. Now, she was watching them get married and have children. They were moving on with their lives, enjoying success and happiness in marriage. Why did her life have to be so different? Why was she the unlucky one? She'd always lived a virtuous life. She had followed the rules. She'd been faithful to God. Why did she have to be the disappointment? The rejected failure?

She hated their pity and indignant looks. They treated her like some orphaned child. Like some pathetic, lost teenager struggling to find her way through life. However, she had not lost her way. She knew who she was. She knew what she wanted. She had not given up on her dreams. Not yet...

Her husband had tried to console her, trying to give emotional stability. He tried to conceal his disappointment, but her condition had caused him to turn to another woman. This other woman was harsh, often ridiculing her because of her affliction. This other woman was able to provide things that she had not been able to give her husband. He still treated her with the same respect and tenderness. She still felt loved and appreciated, but this other woman was something to him that she could never be. However, what this woman could give him was one of the most treasured gifts in their culture. Hannah was suffering because she was barren.

Standing in the interior of the temple, she fell to her knees and silently cried to God. No sound was heard as she secretly wept, pouring out her soul. Perhaps the shame kept her cries inaudible. Perhaps the pain cut too deeply, for when one's heart has been crushed, there are moments when no words will come. She quietly stammered, lifting her face toward Heaven and calling on a God she'd never felt. Her faith was limited at best, but she was trying.

Just when she was reaching an emotional crescendo, something happened. Why is it that when one thinks nothing else can go wrong, it usually does? If the pain of this moment was not enough, as she lay there in silent agony, the priest walked by.

She didn't hear him approach until he spoke, "Woman, what have you been drinking. You shouldn't bring that foolishness into this holy place."

Her mind was immediately filled with the sting of rejection. Why had the priest spoken into her plight and offered no hope? He found her in her lowest moment and offered no solace. What she needed was restitution. What she found was rebuke.

She had never been insulted so badly. How could a man of God, a man called to be compassionate and caring, reprimand her without closer scrutiny? It seemed so unfair, but she summoned the strength to sound un-offended. She muttered,

"I'm sorry, sir. It's not as it appears. I've had nothing to drink. I'm merely a desperate woman in dire need of an answer from God. I'm without a child, and I don't want to remain barren. I've been pouring my heart out, petitioning for a baby."

> **God's blessings are not proof of God's favor.**

The priest, who had not been spiritually sensitive enough to see her pain was at least considerate enough to bless her. He spoke a miracle into her life. Although God was growing frustrated with Eli (personally), He still honored him (positionally). This is a danger that ministry must be aware of. Just because the blessings of God are evident does not mean that God honors the man. We must never mistake results for relationship.

Within a short time, the prophecy came true. Hannah conceived, and after the appropriate time, she had a baby.

COMPASSION AND COMPROMISE

It is almost angering that a woman in her lowest moment found rebuke in the house of God. In this case, it's an early sign of Eli's failure as a priest and an initial indication that he wasn't in tune with God. He was keeping the obligations of running the temple but was losing connection with God. His two sons, Hophni and Phinehas were on location for his debacle. This is interesting, because if anyone needed reprimanding for their actions in the temple, it was those two. They'd been using their position and lineage to their advantage, committing sexual atrocities on the altars. Eli ignored their despicable behavior but chided a broken woman.

This image is infuriating, but how many times is it replayed in the 21st century? From God's view, how many Hannahs have left the church without finding Him because someone offered a shove instead of an embrace?

The reality is that the world has dramatically shifted over the last few years. Liberalism has taken its toll on modern society. It has made its way into the restricted confines of the church. Many people have recognized this spiritual assault and have refused to tolerate its attempts to strangle holiness and purity. However, in strong attempts to defend the church against the relentless and well thought-out attacks of Satan, many fail to remember that this is a spiritual battle, fought on spiritual ground, and never against flesh and blood. Spiritual frustration manifested in the natural realm is never a Godly result. People are destroyed, and the perfect will of God thwarted, by well meaning individuals who cause others to feel rejected. In the aftermath of this satanic sneak attack, the church has struggled to negotiate the difference between compassion and compromise. As man's views have deviated from God's, we cross boundaries that cause the church to become hidden, while God remains unafraid to deal with difficult and problematic people on their terms. God's approach is never to violate a standard, but if He must irritate the pious to help someone in need, He doesn't hesitate.

> **We must not fear compromise so profoundly that we close our minds to compassion.**

The church lives by priorities, precedence, and position: God lives by principle. He'll never violate eternal principle for man's priorities. He isn't concerned with position from a top down approach. With God, the last shall be first. He looks from the bottom up. God isn't apprehensive about setting precedence. If He's in need of something that doesn't exist, He creates it. If He encounters unsolved problems, He opens dispensations, unlocks closed doors, and begins ministries.

Jesus allowed an impure prostitute to touch a rabbi. He touched lepers, spoke to the unclean, and dined with sinners. He was always more worried about people than precedence.

God isn't concerned with human priorities. This is tricky,

because we should have priorities. However, when natural priorities hinder the will of God, they are wrong. The danger with priorities is that it's far too easy to turn lists into laws, and nothing keeps men from the will of God like the laws they have created. There are times God bring supernatural works, but cutting through the red tape of religion is difficult, even for God.

He would not do many mighty works there because of their unbelief (Matthew 13:58).

Many new converts become frustrated because they violated no principle of God's Word, but are still ostracized by long-term believers. Some people are filled with the Holy Ghost, baptized in Jesus name, and have repented of their sins. They've been committed to the church for months. However, they're still limited by the congregation, not out of growth or wisdom (those are natural parts of the process), but because of how they look based on previous decisions before conversion. Unfortunately, for these new converts, there are saints who arrogantly tie their leader's hands by causing trouble if the appearance of those in the church doesn't meet their expectations. Good pastors can become frustrated because they have to choose between new babies feeling isolated and old saints concerned with compromise. The truth is that wherever rapid growth occurs, not everyone is going to appear holy and acceptable. That is why God said,

You must not call unclean what God has already cleansed (Acts 10:15).

There is an ultra thin line between compassion and compromise, but Jesus chose to err on the side of compassion when it came to people in desperate need of Him. He met the woman caught in the act of adultery. There's no indication that He clothed her properly before speaking with her. No doubt she still had the stench of sin and the appearance of her lustful lifestyle on her body. Her outward appearance broke principle in every way possible. However, Jesus looked into the heart of a woman who was terrified, broken, and lost. He addressed that first, prioritizing her lost soul over the church members that were ready to throw stones. That is Jesus. He fights to protect those in need. He defends the guilty. We must not be so afraid of compromise that we lose all sense of compassion.

To clarify: I am not advocating that a church remove its standards or desire for holiness in order to become more attractive to sinners. I am saying that if the church is apostolic in nature, it will be attractive to sinners. I am also stating that new people should feel safe and comfortable in our churches. God should be given the time to lead people to the truth, allowing the change come from the inside out. The pastor of an assembly should be given the right to pastor, not having to worry about the saints trying to get people in line with the doctrine of the assembly. God's purpose is to radically save people from hell, not just change their dress code. An appearance change does not affect any other part of a man. However, a heart changes filters down to every other part of a man's life. We should allow God to captivate a person's heart.

At times, there are issues with new converts that must be addressed. Being new does not give one the right to willingly violate the principles of God's Word or foundation doctrines of a church. One cannot expect to be fully used in a congregation if unwilling to conform to the key beliefs of the church. Wisdom demands that growth occur before new converts take on major responsibilities. The church body should trust the pastor to set those limits. After all, the souls in the congregation are his responsibility.

Compromise is a legitimate threat that must be guarded against. We must fight to preserve Christian virtues and Godly principles of holiness. In a world unifying to remove and isolate God, we must distance ourselves from the spirit of the end-time further than ever before. We must not lose our identity in attempts to become more relevant and socially acceptable. However, there's a time and place for every battle. Hurting new babies who have violated no Scriptural principle is not the arena in which to combat the spirit of compromise.

MISGUIDED LOYALTY

The man lay awake, staring into the dim candle. He had too many thoughts pulsing through his mind. His position demanded much of him. He had so many duties that men of lessor standing did not have. It wasn't like any of them could be taken lightly. In his world, if one neglected these ancient duties, he could end up being pulled from the tabernacle by a rope.

However, tonight he was concerned about more than his duties. He'd known about the trouble his sons had been causing. Their hearts were full of pride. They were becoming a hindrance to the kingdom of God, leading many astray by following their own lusts. The blind eye he'd been casting in his sons' direction was wrong. He'd heard the rumors more than once. Several of the elders were gravely offended. God couldn't be pleased. He should execute judgment harshly and swiftly. Anyone else would've long since been punished, but this was his flesh and blood. It was too difficult to execute a guilty verdict.

Suddenly, he shivered. What was the feeling that had just passed, stirring up long forgotten memories. He thought he'd felt a shimmer of what had once been. A feeling so forgotten that it was no longer fully discernible. A brief recognition that the atmosphere was slightly altered.

Eli quickly brushed it from his mind and lay his head back down to sleep. Hopefully, the fatigue would overtake him, and he'd have a peaceful night. Maybe he could dream of places he'd never seen and remember feelings once held dear. As he closed his eyes, he thought he heard someone speak from the distance darkness, but clearly it was his imagination.

In another part of the house, a young child restlessly slept. He had resisted as long as possible, watching the shadows from the flickering candle dance across the wall in contorting shapes and sizes. For a while, he had imagined what each shadow could be. After he could withstand the oncoming slumber no longer, he gently closed his eyes and fell into a deep rest.

He tossed and turned from one position to the next, subconsciously repositioning in an attempt to get more comfortable. He usually had no trouble sleeping. Why was tonight different? Nothing out of the ordinary had occurred. He had been feeling quite well before he'd slipped into bed and pulled the soft sheets around him. He'd fallen asleep amidst distant memories of a woman he hadn't seen in a while and a jacket that was now too small to wear.

His life was certainly odd. He'd never fit in with the other men in this dysfunctional family. They were older. He was remarkably perceptive for his age and had quickly learned that many of the elders looked down on the other boys. He had never discovered why.

He did wonder why he wasn't like most children his age. They got to romp and play, frivolously wasting time and enjoying the niceties of childhood. He wasn't that lucky. He was learning the routines, customs, and traditions of the church. He didn't mind. Somehow, he knew that he was learning something that would make a monumental difference one day. However, for tonight he was tucked in bed, a little child with big dreams.

Suddenly, he sat up, every fiber of his tiny frame on edge. Panic stricken, he scanned the room for movement. He knew he was in a holy place. Nothing vile or evil could enter. So, why was he afraid?

The iridescent glow from the stick of melting wax made the room eerily lonely. The dancing silhouettes that had appeared to be funny people moving to some comedic song, now seemed like monsters that shouldn't be dwelling in this sacred place. That thought did little to ease his racing mind.

There was something else in the room, something

otherworldly. The scariest part wasn't that he felt its presence now. The worst part was what had awakened him. He had been provoked from his sleep because someone had distinctly called his name.

Overcoming his innate fears and forcing himself to think logically, he did something that no young child ever wants to when possibly confronted by the proverbial boogieman. He slowly pulled down the covers, freeing himself to move. Mustering up his courage, Samuel leapt from the bed and ran into the prophet's room.

"Eli," he nervously muttered, "Did you call for me?"

"No, Samuel. I did not say anything. You must be dreaming. Go back to bed," Eli sleepily muttered.

Samuel returned, but sleep was far from his mind. He knew it had not been a dream. Something had called to him from the darkness.

Twice more this process continued. The old man struggled to sit up, his weight making it difficult to shift quickly without losing his breath. After a few disgruntled moments of trying to view Samuel through the darkness, something finally clicked Eli's sleep-deprived brain. Since he'd been so far removed from God with this young child's mother, it would seem that he would've been more connected concerning the lad. However, instead of growing more in tune, he had become more isolated from God. The tragedy is that Eli was too intoxicated with sleep to contemplate why God was speaking to a child instead of the chosen priest.

He groggily spoke to the boy, "Next time you hear your name, speak into the darkness and ask the voice to continue talking. Tell it that you will listen."

The hinges on the bed creaked disapproving, as the old prophet uninterestingly lowered his corpulent frame down again. Nervously, a young Samuel approached the darkness, this time preparing to speak.

Later, it awakened him. He did as Eli had suggested, and God introduced Himself to Samuel for the first time. Into the stillness, God spoke judgment upon the house of Eli, promised Samuel that he would walk in Heaven's anointing and do a marvelous work for the Kingdom. Samuel knew that he was too young to grasp what was being revealed, but he also knew that this moment was monumental.

As God spoke the last words, Samuel felt a warmth he had never encountered. As the voice of God disappeared down the dark corridors of the temple, Samuel sat alone, contemplating everything he'd heard.

The darkness slowly faded, dim light making the distorted images around the room more clear. Somewhere, a lone bird resonated his solitary song into the crisp morning air, while the lamp of God was extinguished in the temple.

Eli's eyes had gone dim. His Godly vision had been disrupted the moment he knew of his sons' transgressions and ignored them. Allowing his sons to dishonor God couldn't be permitted. Therefore, God began to work in an unorthodox manner. He spoke through a child that wasn't of priestly lineage.

Eli is the poster-boy for someone who was in the right place, had the right teachings, had the blessings of the lineage, but was too caught up in his flesh to be spiritually aware of what was going on. He missed the opportunity to develop Samuel into the man his sons had never been. He failed to work the blessings he could've bestowed on the Kingdom. God had to work around Eli rather than through him. This is the greatest tragedy of someone who claims to be in love with God. Let it never be said that God had to perform His will despite me.

Today, it's astonishing how often this is the case. God has saved many people in spite of every attempt from some in the church to sabotage His efforts. There are those who find every fault possible against new people coming into the church. They live to "fix" everything that's broken in those around them. They have constructed beams in their own eyes from the splinters they've pulled out of the eyes of others. However, this beam has been constructed so privately that they don't even realize the depth of their own destructive behavior. Eli had no clue that God was paying attention, until a child came to him with a stinging indictment from Heaven.

At first, the church should focus more inwardly than outwardly. It must not be known for judgmental attitudes toward those who are different. External judgment is always deadly, for it allows one to ignore the damaged fruit of their own carnality. Compromise is a legitimate threat, but compassion must be realized if people are going to be effectively reached for the Kingdom of God.

Eli set precedence the moment he ignored his sons' evil ways. He accepted their weak excuses. He condemned a lonely woman for drinking in the house of God, yet it was acceptable for his sons to commit whoredom on the altar. His priorities were way out of line. He allowed his sons' position to keep him from forcing them into public reprimand. However, God wasn't as protective when it came to precedence. He wasn't concerned about what had happened beforehand. God wasn't concerned with politics or positions. He certainly didn't care about human priorities. He chose a child who was given by his mother to the church. This child had no birthright, no lineage, no heritage, therefore no rightful claim. However, God decided that he was the right candidate for the job because he was in tune enough to listen and smart enough to draw near. The late Bishop Murrell Ewing powerfully stated that the secret to hearing is to get as close to the speaker as possible. God is still looking for those two requirements. Will you hear? Will you respond?

God is not interested in the bitter ramblings of those who have lost the zeal of their relationship. God killed an entire generation that wouldn't stop murmuring while escaping from bondage to the land of spiritual promise. A wise elder once asked me,

"Do you know how you can tell if a person is sold out to God?"

The answer was astounding. How much do they complain? If they are living for the Kingdom, the imperfections and problems of life are secondary to the plans of God. Are we willing to sacrifice for others who are lost? Are we willing to allow mercy and grace to operate?

As Christians, everyone isn't on the same level. Therefore, we cannot judge spirituality by observable means alone. That's why God examines the heart. God knows more and sees further than we can. Perhaps He should be given the opportunity to operate in a person's life the way He sees fit.

THE THIN LINE

Adam set sin in motion by succumbing to Eve's wishes and eating the forbidden fruit. However, from the moment Adam fell, God was already working to redeem man and restore the severed relationship. Interwoven in the punishment that God pronounced on both Adam and Eve were promises that man and God would be reunited.

To Eve, He discussed the pain of childbirth. *In pain you will bring forth children.* The process would hurt, but the result ends in fruitfulness. God also promised that, from that fruitfulness, a child would come who would bruise the head of the serpent.

God told Adam that he would be forced to work by the sweat of his brow. Adam would die. However, something transpired in the midst of this curse that had spoken to Adam on a deeper level. God had pronounced judgment and death, yet the next verse says,

"And Adam called his wife's name Eve, for she was the mother of all living," (Genesis 3:20).

Apparently, Adam had an understanding that although everything was bleak and negative in the moment, time and grace would ensure that the existing fissure would one day be closed.

As the angel removed Adam and Eve from the garden, life would prove cruel. Adam's transgressions didn't take long to take their toll on his family. The couple's first son, Cain, killed their second son, Abel. God had been pleased with Abel's sacrificial offering but not Cain's. Cain felt the sting of rejection and instead of changing his gift, he had decided to murder Abel.

Not much has changed over the last few thousand years. Those blessed enough to be called His people, are often some of the most jealous people on the planet. Within the church, people are murdered through gossip, lies, and casual conversation with the same veracity as those in the world. Kingdom-minded men and women aren't concerned about glory or credit and remove themselves from the political arena. However, these outstanding men and women are often at the mercy of those who are not so Kingdom-minded and continue to pursue their own agendas. If not careful, the enemy wants the church to become a place that promotes workplace hostility through competitive reinforcement.

The church has never been an "every man for himself" environment. Cain failed to understand this principle, doing what most people do when confronted with the futility of their own humanity. He lashed out at the one who had succeeded where he had failed. Cain slew Abel, and God wasn't pleased with what took place. The first murder occurred between brothers just one generation removed from the tragic fall in the garden. Had Adam and Eve known that their mistake would lead to the damnation and banishment of their eldest son and the murder of their youngest, they would have been more careful about falling into the snare of sin so willingly.

However, here they stood, mourning the death of their second born. God approached Cain, and His approach is particularly intriguing. He had once approached Adam much the same way… With a question. Adam had hid from God, detailing the result of someone living under condemnation of the flesh. God asked Adam,

"Where are YOU?"

God approached Cain much the same way. Unlike Adam, Cain did not merely make a poor choice. He symbolized someone who has imitated spiritual perfection while championing his own agenda. He had made sacrifices and communed with God. He and Abel had the same upbringing, but when God examined both, He found Cain lacking. Cain wasn't spiritually up to par, and this fact angered him. However, Cain didn't respond like Adam had. Cain didn't physically flee. He went about business as usual, pretending that he had no care in the world.

God showed up and spoke to Cain, asking him a question, just as He had started the ill-fated conversation with Adam so many years before. However, the topic of this question was different. He asked Adam, "Where are YOU." God asked the church going, pretender Cain, "Where is YOUR BROTHER?"

God demands that His church look outward. The measuring stick of right standing in the Kingdom is how connected we are with the whereabouts of others. Cain thought God would forget Abel and focus on what Cain could bring to the table. However, God will never allow someone to elevate his own status at the expense of others.

If not careful, current church culture delineates from God's plan by basing promotion on talent, appeal, popularity, friendship, pedigree, personality, and past performances alone. God promotes from anointing and character. God's main concern was that Cain look outward. Cain obviously had a serious issue with this and was banished from the Kingdom.

The issue with current trends of evangelism is that if a church isn't in constant growth mode, people continually evaluate what's wrong. Forgotten is the fact that church growth cycles between seasons of intense work followed by times of bountiful harvest, just as God prophesied to Adam.

"You will toil. You will reap."

However, because the church isn't continually growing, there's often pressure from within to make church more appealing to the world. This thought isn't harmful, and may at times even prove useful in getting people to attend a local assembly. However, this mentality is extremely dangerous, because it opens the doors for talent and personality searches. As time marches on, placement of people becomes less about anointing and more about natural ability. At times, we are misguided because we allow the politics of religion and influence of people to override divine authority. We were never called to be political. Yet, we unknowingly encourage people to build their own kingdoms. If not careful, the church will fail for not allowing God to promote whom He desires. Also, many young ministers fail to move forward in faith because they seek promotion or affirmation from people around them. If it doesn't come, they feel discouraged and often give up, failing to understand that if God has called a man, that is all the confirmation he will ever need.

On the other side, it is also dangerous for a church to remain stagnant by claiming they are in the planting season. Sowing that doesn't produce a harvest is a definite indication that something is prohibiting God's law from actively working. This should cause God's people to introspective to discover what is hindering the will of God.

The danger of Christianity is that the flesh can be religiously recognized and rewarded, as long as it's done under certain guidelines. It's obvious that one cannot gain recognition in the church if operating under a worldly manifesto. Therefore, anyone desiring to promote their own agenda has to play by church rules. They have to reach others to gain attention. They have to pray to be considered spiritual. They must worship to be taken seriously. They must walk the walk of real Christianity to have validity. If they are going to be a fashionable man or woman of God, there's a certain appearance that must be upheld.

The danger is that this environment makes self-deception far too easy. It is too easy for a man's actions to appear right while his motives are dead wrong. God isn't pleased with such living. However, this behavior isn't only allowed, but encouraged when decisions are based on natural talent and abilities alone. The church must learn to recognize true spirituality through the fruits that are being exemplified.

God responded to Cain, "Your brothers blood is crying to me from the ground."

Blood was speaking condemnation and judgment into the life of Cain. This line of blood was powerful, for it separated Cain from God and found him unworthy of the Kingdom.

. . .

The stranger cowered in fear, as the massive crowd swelled and chanted for the criminal beside him to be punished. These men and women normally possessed some sense of civil virtue. However, at this time, they were ravenous, screaming at the top of their lungs for justice to prevail. They were demanding that this immoral bigot be killed.

The stranger wondered what this man had done to entice the crowd to such malicious behavior. However, he was too afraid to ask, for fear they'd recognize him as a foreigner and harass him in their rage. He didn't want to stand out, being grateful that for once he wasn't the focus of the racial pressure and violence.

The people in the town square began to move, scattering like scared children running from a villainous monster coming from the wilderness. They were still enraged at the controversial figure that had created such commotion, but they were pausing their riot to clear a way for the advancing army marching toward them. Soldiers hurriedly marched through the scurrying crowd, forcing everyone out of the way.

One elderly woman couldn't move fast enough. A

passing soldier shoved her to the ground. A kindhearted young man rushed in to help her escape the stomping of more advancing boots. Children ran ahead of the soldiers, playing with wooden swords, pretending to be in the midst of a fantastical war. They were so engrossed in their games that they failed to understand that there was no honor here. These men were beasts, shoving and pulling, whipping and punching, cursing their way through the mob with merciless intent.

Finally, the stranger saw what had created the stir. A few feet in front of him, in the midst of the Roman guard, was a lone man being bullied through the street. The stranger's heart momentarily stopped at the terrible image of the injured man before him. He'd been beaten beyond recognition. His facial features were swollen and caked with blood, sweat, and tears.

The stranger felt nauseous, as he saw the man's back. Strips of flesh fell like tattered ribbons, revealing open wounds from jagged rips through his skin. How was this man still breathing? What he'd been through would've already crushed most men. The stranger's eyes met those of the beaten victim for just a moment, but the stranger felt a sudden warmth he'd never experienced. Who was this man who had stirred his soul by simply glancing into his eyes?

He wanted to look away from this gruesome scene, but his eyes wouldn't do what his brain desperately demanded. He was about to turn away, when the lone man stumbled, dropping the heavy wooden beams He'd been carrying. The stranger wanted to help him, to reach out his hand, but fear paralyzed him, keeping him on the outskirts, watching helplessly, as this tragedy continued to unfold. However, his inactivity was short-lived, for the a guard grabbed him, pulling him into the chaotic scene.

"You... Pick it up... Carry it for Him."

Simon looked down at the wooden beams forming the shape of a cross. He'd seen this many times before, the dead or dying littering the streets as warnings to others considering revolting against the laws of Rome.

Simon wanted no part in this. He just wanted to be away from this madness. However, if he didn't obey, he'd be killed along with this Man, and death was something he desperately wanted to avoid.

> **Jesus always goes before those willing to mingle their own blood with His, those willing to carry His cross.**

Simon looked again at the beams. My the blood. It had stained every fiber of the boards, soaking into the grain and resting in every crevice. He didn't want to touch it. However, as the soldier violently stepped toward him, Simon stooped down, took the cross in his arms, and lifted it onto his shoulder. As he stood, the heavy cross fell hard against him. A splinter penetrated deep into his skin, ramming through all three layers of his flesh. He felt a strange sensation flood his body, failing to realize that the blood of deity now flowed through his veins, as a drop of the precious blood of Jesus entered his bloodstream.

As he stood with cross in arms, Jesus lifted Himself back to His feet. He looked again into the eyes of Simon, sending chills into the innermost part of Simon's soul. Then, Jesus stepped out to walk in front of him, for Jesus always goes before those willing to mingle their blood with His, those willing to carry His cross.

Jesus went to Calvary and sacrificed His life, taking man's place on the altar, carrying man's guilt and sin, and giving Himself for it. As His holy side was pierced, blood and water flowed to the ground. Once again, blood began to speak. This time the it spoke, not in condemnation of man's guilt, but in man's defense. It spoke concerning God's desire to seek and save those who are lost, to reach into impossible places and save the un-savable. God's ardent desire for redemption was demonstrated as He gave His own life and spilled His own blood to redeem us forever.

Today, there are only two choices concerning the blood. It either speaks condemnation and judgment or grace and mercy. There's still a thin, red line separating compassion and compromise, mercy and mediocrity, grace and godliness. That line is the blood of Jesus Christ.

Prisons With Stained Glass Windows

3
THE KEY AND THE DOOR

The dark, surreptitious spirits behind the downward spiral of Christian virtues have relentlessly warred to ensure that faith, love, and hope are dead. If faith remains, Christians will not stop pursuing the apostolic promises of power and authority that wreck hell's kingdom, destroying its end-time agenda. Faith shields the believer from Satan's idle threats and empty roars, extinguishing the fiery darts before they unleash their poison. Faith is the hymn behind which most Christians march, eyes fixed forward, ever advancing into the cesspool of sin to save ravaged and damaged souls. Fear and intimidation do not intimidate those fastened to faith, refusing to relinquish the ground they've forcefully taken in previous battles. If the underworld's feline wishes to snarl into the sanctums of the holy, his roar is reduced to a purr when faith has convinced the believer that Judah's lion is present. The enemy has launched an all out assault against faith, for as faith dwindles, so does the destiny of the apostolic movement.

Love is also being targeted, as long as true love is present in the heart of the Christian, no lost soul is safe in hell's clutches. As long as love's pulse emanates from the bosom of God, echoing through the hearts of the holy, every sinner is a candidate for redemption. Nothing is lost, and no one is outside of the ever-reaching, fully extended hand of God. Where love exists, the church is ever fighting to regain the lives of those living in legal bondage to the wiles of Satan.

Hope is pushed to succumb to the incessant deluge of darkness battling for supremacy in every realm of human existence. As long as there is breath, hope exists, and the enemy attempts to annihilate every faction of hope from true believers. If hope is not lost, the pressure applied to this earth by satanic influence is weakened, leaving Christians unswayed by the intolerable injustices permeating a culture once rooted in the message of Christ. Hope, love, and faith are three virtues that must remain steadfast if the insurmountable onslaught of hell is going to be driven back and defeated by an apostolic church.

THE KEY

He knelt in humbled posture as he often did during his times of daily devotion. He was accustomed to hearing the voice of God with clarity and immense purpose. This morning had proven different. The usual, tranquil presence which he was accustomed to felt atypical now. As the presence of the Lord engulfed the atmosphere, he felt threatened and abnormally smaller than usual. There was a new tension in the air.

He was by no means a casual man of God. He'd grown accustomed to the near unsympathetic attitude that God displayed at times. However, this was different. There was almost anger emanating into the room. He wanted to hide. He knew that he had done nothing wrong, but the terror he felt was the result of something sinister.

Suddenly, God began to speak. The lucidity of the language was indescribable. He grasped the conveyed emotion behind every word. For what seemed like an eternity, the powerful presence boomed into the stillness. Each word echoed like thunder through a valley. The man shuttered at the consequent actions he would have to take. This was a task better left undone by a man in his position. However, when God charges one to carry a message, the message must be delivered, regardless of the emotional state of the courier.

He listened, as the last word was spoken. A chill overtook the atmosphere, as the warmth of God's presence left the room. He lingered for a few moments, hoping the presence would return, releasing him from the responsibility he'd been given. To his disappointment, no second speech came. The mind of God had been made, and like it or not, the message would have to be relayed.

Later, he stood outside the door leading to the inner courts. Closing his eyes, he took a deep breath, rehearsing the words in his head one last time. Mumbling a quick prayer, he burst into the inner courts. When delivering a message of such brazen significance, he could not do so passively. The very nature of the task demanded an audacious approach. The guards immediately moved forward to detain him. The shocked expressions from the politicians and parliamentarians spoke volumes about his unexpected intrusion. However, almost as quickly as they had moved to hinder his approach, the guards recognized him and awkwardly stepped aside. What were they to do when trapped between allegiance to king and prophet?

Loudly, the voice of the prophet rattled the nervous silence.

"God is not happy about what's been taking place. Your city is going to waste. It's becoming desolate and barren. Many of the citizens are dying, not by fighting to defend their freedom, but from famine and disease. Your leaders have fled like cowards. Many of your supposedly brave warriors were captured and gave up the fight without resistance. The sound of chariots and horses came. The semblance of war made you cower in fear. You took measures to ensure you had enough water. You built a cistern and a means to defend it. You had well thought out plans. You gathered weapons from the armory, taking proper steps to ensure your safety. However, in all your programs and planning, you failed to confer with the only council that truly mattered. You planned everything, but you planned out God.

The prophet took a deep breath before continuing. "However, despite your arrogance, God was merciful and offered a second chance. He demanded retribution because you arrogantly followed your own desires. He wanted you to humble yourself in sackcloth and ashes. He wanted you to shave your heads in remorse and return to placing him first in your life. However, you decided that you'd ride the wave of His goodness until the end. If the enemy overtook you, you figured you'd have had your fleshly fun before you fell. Your priority was on pleasing yourself instead of looking toward the eternal purpose of your God."

The prophet let his words linger in the air. It was not a pause for effect. It was a slight chance to catch his breath again. He had bellowed the words and was feeling parched as he stood in the awkward silence. He looked around, as most of the men looked toward the ground. Others had almost turned away altogether, hiding their shame and fear. The prophet searched the room, his eyes at one point locking with the powerful stare of the king. The king's steel gaze was not broken. However, in the corners of his eyes was a slight wrinkle, perhaps a tiny furrowing of the eyebrows. The usually composed king displayed the smallest hint of concern.

The prophet continued his visual investigation until his eyes locked on the intended target. It was too late to go back now. This was the heart of the message.

"You will never be forgiven for this sin," he shouted, looking coldly into the eyes of the second most prominent person in the room. As they intently stared at each other, the prophet bellowed once again,

"You're the organizer and planner of everything that takes place here. God has seen your arrogance, and for that, He will judge you. He's removing you from your position, stripping you of your honor and reputable name, and removing your royal position. God is not just banishing you in a gentle way. He is angry. He will uproot and humiliate you, pulling you up by your hair to drag you around the room. He will kick you, beat you, and hurl you into a barren and desolate land. He'll leave you there to die. You're a disgrace to the Kingdom...

...What's more, God is going to appoint someone else to take your place. He'll wear your royal robes. He'll be honored with your reputation. He'll be given the highest respect in the kingdom. He'll have the greatest authority, for he will carry the king's seal. What he opens will be opened, and what he closes will be closed. You had it all, but you're being destroyed because of your feelings of self-importance. Now, he'll have the greatest honor bestowed upon him. His honor will be so immense that the lowest member of his family will reap its rewards. He'll be given the key of the house of David. He'll be driven by God like a nail in a sure place, able to stand in perilous times."

His job finished, the immense task complete, Isaiah turned and boldly walked from the room, leaving behind a highly concerned King Hezekiah, and an arrogant Secretary of State, soon to be removed, Shebna.

SHEBNA

One of the greatest tragedies in Scripture is the colossal collapse of the house of Shebna. The calamity that Israel endured as a result of his powerful reign under King

Hezekiah is soundly noted. However, the depiction of the state of Israel at this time sounds eerily similar to the status of mainstream Christianity today.

God was upset that Israel had turned to programs and planning for protection instead of consulting Him. Today, the enemy knows his time is short; therefore, he is unleashing a frenzied attack on the infrastructure of the apostolic movement. Youthful leadership is often arrogant and mistakenly walks away from doctrinal mandates that have been the salvation, protection, and power of the apostolic movement for decades. Most people are not lost to the strength and deadly deception of the devil. Often, people abandon their relationship with God merely because they are in the midst of a spiritual famine. Numerous "believers" walk away from Truth because they hear the approaching sounds of war without the overwhelming assurance that God has not abandoned us in time of greatest need.

The most well thought out plans didn't impress God. He was upset that He wasn't consulted first. Water was the source of life. Under Shebna's leadership, the people drew inward, protecting the source to ensure that the well didn't dry up. Instead of flowing outward, the water supply was redirected inward to create a surplus that was easier to defend against invading armies.

Today, the source of life is highly guarded. The tendency is to protect the church against the invasion of perverseness, at times to the point of drawing inward, making the wells of living water only accessible to those living inside the protective walls of religiosity. The stance toward outwardly confronting the onslaught of Satan is difficult, for the church as a whole is more concerned with enhancing its membership and less concerned with reaching the lost. The church has become more of a building than a body.

> **Jesus remains locked in prisons with stained-glass windows, as we leave Him within the safe walls of our buildings.**

The introduction of cathedrals and the construction of church buildings over the past few centuries have made the church more localized. As a result, most Christians practice the deepest forms of Christianity in prisons with stained-glass windows, forever locking God into the confines of their local assembly. The tabernacle was never meant to be a restrictive barrier, keeping believers from acting out their beliefs in un-churched society. The well was never meant to flow inward. Once again, the church must shift its view toward the world that Christ loved enough to die for.

The most dangerous attribute of Shebna is his name. Shebna means, *he who rests and is made captive*. What an indictment and foreshadowing nightmare. His name breaks open the dilemma that comes with resting on the laurels of religion. Resigning the call out of fear, failure, intimidation, stress, fatigue, or any other fleshly concern is foolish. Abandoning the anointing of the apostolic church is futile. The war rages; the enemy sneakily shifts; deception develops, and wickedness is cultivated; all while the church silently battles to stay awake. Stagnant pools of what used to be tributaries roaring from Heaven's seas serve as visual reminders of what happens when the anointing takes respite from waging war on darkness. Tired soldiers find that the battle is easier while steadfastly marching. Once the feet rest and the eyelids close, the durable warrior finds that marching an inconvenience. Many are lost, not by some demonic sword on the spiritual battlefront of the mind, but by surrendering without a fight, because they chose to stop and relax a while.

At times, even the most dedicated disciple needs a break. Every one should occasionally step away from responsibility and take a vacation. That's not the break being referenced.

Shebna took a break from reality. He allowed his own superciliousness to alter the perception of his importance to the kingdom. He began working his own plans, making the primary purpose of God a fading memory. His methods and programs were meticulously planned. He was an organizer, proficient with finances, and adept at recognizing and manipulating the local landscape. He was a revolutionary leader.

Revolutionary leaders are necessary to navigate the abysmal muddle of the 21st Century. The Kingdom of God needs men of intellect who know how to do more than preach. Ministers must know how to lead. Education is more pertinent today than at any other time. There's no requirement of secular degree to be used in God's kingdom. However, some working knowledge of ministry, people, communication, finances, and the Word of God is an added commodity. The more one knows about leadership principles, the better he or she is equipped to lead. However, the pitfall of radical leadership is the tendency to believe that progress and success are more about the leader than God. If a church is to be apostolic, this can never be, for God will share His glory with no one, and without His glory apostolic power and authority cannot exist.

Despite God's warning that pride always precedes destruction, many modern leaders still persist in their own knowledge while endeavoring to navigate the perilous waters of current evangelism. Growing the Kingdom has never been so mentally challenging. The sad reality is that the more emotionally taxing it becomes, the less we move toward spiritual principles, and the more we've been engulfed by professionalism.

The prevailing mentality sweeping this age is that being spiritual doesn't work. We must resort to natural principles engineered by the finest intellectuals on the forefront of Christian sociology. However, it's not that spiritual principles have failed, as much as how they are utilized.

Prayer, as a means to dominate God and demand He respond to our desires has failed. Prayer is not a means to an end. It is the source of apostolic power, not because it forces God to act, but because it intimately connects us to Him, enabling us to act under His authority. Fasting has become a crutch to bring on revival or the restoration of lost souls, instead of a powerful weapon against the flesh. Fasting demands the death of self and the continual diminishing of one's carnality. This is of utmost importance, for flesh that is not shrinking is growing. True fasting is a foundational element of the apostolic movement, because by sacrificing self on the altar of Godly passion, we remove the fleshly barriers that keep God from sitting on the throne of the human heart. Until God is replaced as the head of one's life, that person can never walk in the fullness of revelation and Godly influence that epitomizes the apostolic tradition.

Worship as a means to get God to fix problems and defeat enemies is the antithesis of why those at the origin of Pentecostalism worshipped Him. Worship, from a motive of receiving instead of giving will never produce apostolic authority.

The dilemma is that God does respond to the praise of His people. We often mistake this response as approval for how we have entered His presence. However, receiving natural benefits and walking in a book of Acts anointing are two different issues.

The main matter of spirituality failing the church is rooted in the way the church body has interpreted its own role in the spiritual process. Spiritual function has replaced actual relationship, and that has led to the weakening of the church's infrastructure. A church that supernaturally dominates the darkness cannot exist independent of a relationship with God. Relationship is still the defining characteristic of the true church's culture.

Shebna rested and was led captive. The sadness of this unfolding scenario is that Shebna was bound and not even aware. He thought he was working on behalf of God when God's views were altogether different. Those in the Kingdom felt that Shebna was leading them in the right direction, but God was demanding far greater from him. Even King Hezekiah was pleased with what Shebna had been accomplishing, but God's opinion is the only one that matters.

The Bible is full of instances where God warns, at times even pleads with His people to wake up from their slumber to live in the powerful dimension that He intended. Romans 13:11-14 says:

> 11-*And that, knowing the time, that now it is high time to awake out of sleep: for now is our salvation nearer than when we believed.*
>
> 12 -*The night is far spent, the day is at hand: let us therefore cast off the works of darkness, and let us put on the armor of light.*
>
> 13 -*Let us walk honestly, as in the day; not in rioting and drunkenness, not in chambering and wantonness, not in strife and envying.*
>
> 14 -*But put ye on the Lord Jesus Christ, and make not provision for the flesh, to fulfill the lusts thereof.*

> 1- *Awake, awake; put on thy strength, O Zion; put on thy beautiful garments, O Jerusalem, the holy city: for henceforth there shall no more come into thee the uncircumcised and the unclean.*
>
> 2- *Shake thyself from the dust; arise, and sit down, O Jerusalem: loose thyself from the bands of thy neck, O captive daughter of Zion.*
>
> 3- *For thus saith the Lord, Ye have sold yourselves for*

naught; and ye shall be redeemed without money.

Isaiah 52:1-3

14-Wherefore he saith, Awake thou that sleepest, and arise from the dead, and Christ shall give thee light.

15-See then that ye walk circumspectly, not as fools, but as wise,

16-Redeeming the time, because the days are evil.

17-Wherefore be ye not unwise, but understanding what the will of the Lord is.

Ephesians 5:14-17

God desires a church that will move into His promises. Anointing, power, miracles, signs, and wonders await those who recognize the danger of resting. God is only interested in people who refuse to become captive to their own intuitions and ideas. He still wants His church to become the mighty army He died to create.

God is so powerful that he led captivity captive (Ephesians 4:8). The spirits battling to imprison Him were themselves imprisoned. Anything short of that is failure. It's impossible to possess a true relationship with God while remaining in bondage. It's impossible for sin to remain undetected in an apostolic church. It's impossible for a passionate, apostolic church to fail at reaching the lost. It's impossible for a community to remain unaffected by an anointed, apostolic church.

> **Has the church become apostolic in name but not in power?**

Is it possible that the church is not realizing the benefits of its apostolic nature? Could that be because we are apostolic in name only? Is it possible that many churches have made the mistake of overestimating its true spiritual impact because we look toward naturalistic concepts? Why have the gifts of the Spirit dwindled in many apostolic churches? The greatest tragedy of the apostolic movement would be for a church to be bound and defeated without being aware.

The Key to apostolic anointing and authority is to refuse the way of Shebna. Ingenuity, wisdom, leadership, programs, and talent will never be able to bring the power and demonstration that the latter-day church should exhibit. The spirit of self-reliance must be defeated or the church is destined to live with marginal power, making little difference in people's lives. Humility, selflessness, and sacrifice are the keys to unlocking spiritual promises, propelling the church into the purpose that Christ propagated through His passionate teaching and life. As long as man feels he can bring change without God, he'll remain bound by the obstacles and opposition that have always ruled him. As long as man fails to change the climate of defeat and failure because of a fascination with numerical and financial growth, the church will continually deviate from its original purpose, which is apostolic authority that produces permanent change.

THE DOOR

He alertly looked through the darkness of his room and wondered what had awakened him. Everything appeared normal. There were no strange sounds, only a disturbing silence. Nothing was out of place, yet something had definitely alarmed him.

He sat up in bed, shaking the remaining cobwebs from his mind. Something strange was taking place, something he couldn't sleep through. If he didn't know better, he would've thought his life was about to take a positive turn. He didn't know the reason behind the feeling, but whatever had awakened him had left an unexplainable sensation of peace amidst the fear.

As his feet touched the cool floor, his mind wouldn't stop racing. What was happening? His heart felt warm and tender, yet his brain was on high alert. He thought through his steps of the previous day. Nothing out of the ordinary had occurred.

Suddenly, his thoughts were interrupted by a gentle shuffling in the distance. Outside, the sheep were bleating, busily echoing their sentiments to the moon. He quickly dressed, not really sure why. He'd just latched his second sandal when a soft knock on the door interrupted the silence. Quickly removing the board from behind it, he slightly cracked the door to peer outside. He bowed in reverence when the door opened, revealing the mighty prophet Isaiah.

"Eliakim," Isaiah started in a forceful tone, "this is the day your life will change. You've been chosen by God."

Eliakim was the complete opposite of Shebna. Shebna had ruled with little consideration, but Eliakim led with passion and fervor. He was highly concerned with the welfare of others. Those around him recognized and appreciated the difference.

Eliakim was not nearly as recognizable as Shebna, for he rarely promoted himself. His only promotion was for the king, the kingdom, and His God. He was sold out, always loyal, and uncommonly devoted to the tasks he'd been assigned.

Just as with Shebna, the man's name described the nature of His character. His name means, *God will rise*. He was chosen to lead Israel from spiritual captivity to prosperity and promise. However, Eliakim understood that he couldn't do it alone. God would have to rise in order for anything of worth to be accomplished.

With Eliakim, it wasn't about well thought out tactics and perfectly constructed plans. It was about God rising. Eliakim was not into craftily detailing the next adventure to captivate the masses in Jerusalem. He was only concerned with elevating God's fame among the people. He wasn't interested in protecting the water by building cisterns and isolating wells. Drawing the life source inward for easier defense was not his agenda. It was about God being exalted. Financial risks didn't matter. It was about God being in His rightful position. Eliakim was only concerned with bringing in the presence of God.

Eliakim came from the loins of Hilkiah. Hilkiah means *God's portion*. Everything is God's portion. Eliakim had learned from his father that God had been given portion (power and authority) over Jerusalem. Therefore, Eliakim wasn't afraid to rock the boat of tradition or challenge the status quo. Eliakim wanted everyone to quit bickering and get involved. It was all about God rising in their midst. Eliakim still strived for natural excellence but only as a sign that God was worthy of their very best. Above all else, Eliakim wanted God to be in control.

This story beautifully illustrates the relationship between a church rooted in natural excellence with religious overtones and a church that's moved past religion and into relationship.

A "Shebna" church trusts only in its leadership, fine treatment of others, and stirring programs to reach, rescue, and retain the lost. However, programs have proven good at reaching, weak at rescuing, and broken at retaining.

An "Eliakim" church makes plans and has a purpose just like a "Shebna" church, but an "Eliakim" church makes sure that the plans have come from God and not from man. An "Eliakim" church makes sure that God is elevated by every portion of the plan. Accolades are not handed out to men like candy. God is given the glory for everything that is accomplished.

Planning is essential. Reaching people on their own terms is important. Natural excellence is critical. However, the "Eliakim" church balances both, ensuring that natural issues are empowered by the supernatural principles of prayer and fasting, which always leads to intimacy with God. It makes sure that the glory is God's alone. That is the apostolic nature of the Eliakim church.

God's blessings were with Eliakim, while Shebna's methods proved to be unstable and weak. He was eventually removed. However, Eliakim was driven *as a nail in a sure place*. His family was given permanence. His status was forever memorialized in Jewish history. He was the example of what God desires His church to be. He set his face toward His purpose and made sure when he marched into battle, it was with the presence of God. A church grounded in talent, programs, and personal agendas may generate excitement, but it will never survive. A church committed to making Jesus shine in every way possible will last, for permanence attracts people.

The key to apostolic ministry is to possess the attitude of Eliakim. If this is the key to evangelistic authority, then what is the door that leads to end-time movement? What is the entrance into a life of apostolic power?

The book of Revelations reveals that Jesus has been given the *key of the house of David. He opens doors, and they remain opened. He closes doors, and they remain closed (Revelation 3:7).* This prophetic utterance spoken to the leader of the church of Sardis echoes the sentiments detailed in the book of Isaiah concerning Eliakim.

Eliakim was a type and shadow of the Redeemer of the world, Jesus Christ. He came humbly and quietly made a difference. Jesus came into the world humbly, a meager Lamb that had come to die. However, he rose a Lion, the King of kings. The key to apostolic authority, power, and anointing is true submission to the authority that's been placed over one's life.

Without allowing Christ to rise, without placing Him at the forefront again, the church will struggle between two worlds. In one, the church thrives for eternity, because it's established in eternal wisdom, principles, and power. In the other, the church struggles from focusing on natural gains and numerical trends. The attitude and fervor with which one engages the Kingdom alters eternity. Both types of churches exist, but only one is the church that Christ intended.

WHERE IS THIS JESUS?

Jesus often came to people in forms they didn't recognize. After His death, He appeared as a gardener. He appeared to the disciples as a ghost on the raging sea. The men on the Road to Emmaus recognized Him as a stranger until their eyes were opened. Many people found that Jesus didn't fit their cookie cutter mold.

That is still the way of Jesus. How often we come to church and expect God to follow the schedule. How often God alters preconceived ideas by showing up in ways we never imagined. The reality is that God is ready to do a mighty work every time His people gather. At times, we just expect far less than He is willing to perform. Therefore, less is what we receive.

If God is ready to work every time a need is present, then why isn't it happening? Where is He? Where is He when He seems to be hiding? How can I find Him, when He seems so distant? Where are the souls that God desires to reach in every service? Where are the miracles that God desires for the apostolic church? Where is the mighty Spirit of end-time revival?

The answer is easy, but we get it so backwards at times. We think that God shows up because we live righteously. We pay tithes, keep holiness standards, abstain from the world's perversion and filth, and maintain healthy attitudes. We hope that God is present to reward us for our obedience.

However, spiritual portfolios don't impress God. He isn't moved by how worthy we think we are. He doesn't go to church to pat people on the back or pin roses to their chests. His purpose is entirely different.

Jesus goes to church for two reasons only. He goes to receive the worship and praise that He is worthy of, and He goes to meet needs. He said,

"I am not come to call the righteous, but sinners to repentance."

It is also said three times, "The whole have no need of me. I have come for the sick."

Jesus said, "The Son of Man has come to seek and save that which is lost."

He gave us the parables of the lost sheep, lost coin, and prodigal son because He was trying to teach us an immutable truth. The presence of the Lord that the apostolic church searches for will never be found by simply gathering on Sundays, worshipping a few moments, and then going home.

God will show up because He loves praise and worship,

and where two or three people are gathered in His name, He will be there. The danger is that we can enter the periphery of God's presence with this mentality. However, the Word of God has made it exceedingly clear where true revival lies. True revival is not behind the walls made with men's hands. It is not in cathedrals, temples, or church buildings. True revival is in the streets, the grassroots level of where the hungry dwell. Jesus is not waiting behind four walls, glass doors, or stained glass. He is not waiting for the pulpit and pew to ignite. Jesus is where He has always been. He is where the lost and broken are, dwelling among those that others have forgotten. He is among the sick, heavy burdened, depressed, and lonely. That is where we will find Jesus. Truly powerful churches are dynamic only because they've learned to get into their communities. They have learned how to bring the un-churched into God's presence, both in and out of their buildings.

At times, we feel that Jesus has hidden the real power, authority, and anointing from us. We feel that the womb of the church has been temporarily closed. However, it is not concealed at all. Perhaps we've been looking in the wrong places. Jesus left the anointing in plain sight. He was always moved by compassion for people's needs. The miraculous was seldom produced by the whims of the church. It was never the disciples' cries for the supernatural that caused Him to respond.

However, He was moved by one woman in a funeral procession. What the church could not accomplish, one father with a possessed boy did. What the religious could not pray into existence, one man with a withered hand, one blind man at the gate, one woman with an issue of blood, one family in need at a wedding, one group of hungry and thirsty people, and ten lepers accomplished.

The church's notions never moved Jesus. It was the needs of hurting people that moved Him. In His book, God Came Near, Max Lucado summarized this Jesus perfectly:

> "*The tongue that called forth the dead was a human one. That hand that touched the leper had dirt under His nails. The feet upon which the woman wept were calloused and dusty – His tears – oh don't miss those tears – they came from a heart as broken as yours or mine has ever been. So people came to Him – my they came to Him. They came at night. They touched Him as He walked down the street. They followed Him around the sea. They invited Him into their homes and placed their children at His feet. Why? Because He refused to be a statue in a cathedral or a priest in an elevated pulpit. He chose rather to be touchable, approachable, and reachable. He was Jesus.*"

We cry for revival. We long for power and anointing. We cannot wait to see miracles, signs, and wonders. However, we'll be waiting a long time if we remain in the building. If we're truly hungry for the supernatural, we must be more than permanent fixtures in God's house. We too must be approachable, touchable, and reachable. The only way to do that is to become like Jesus and move among the needy. It is far too easy to ignore people if we never place ourselves in position to see their needs.

Jesus indicated exactly where he could be found:

> *Then shall the King say unto them on his right hand, Come, ye blessed of my Father, inherit the kingdom prepared for you from the foundation of the world:*
>
> *For I was an hungred, and ye gave me meat: I was thirsty, and ye gave me drink: I was a stranger, and ye took me in:*
>
> *Naked, and ye clothed me: I was sick, and ye visited me: I was in prison, and ye came unto me.*
>
> *Then shall the righteous answer him, saying, Lord, when saw we thee an hungred, and fed thee? or thirsty, and gave thee drink?*
>
> *When saw we thee a stranger, and took thee in? or naked, and clothed thee?*
>
> *Or when saw we thee sick, or in prison, and came unto thee?*
>
> *And the King shall answer and say unto them, Verily I say unto you, Inasmuch as ye have done it unto one of the least of these my brethren, ye have done it unto me.*
>
> *Matthew 25:34-40*

Jesus wanted the church to understand, the miracles are waiting for you among the broken and hopeless. Healing will be discovered among the sick. The church will find absolute authority and power when it steps among the oppressed. One must get involved with others in order to be apostolic in nature.

Jesus looks for a church that will pursue His passion of going into the world for the Kingdom. Only by engaging the lost will true apostolic ministry be established. Many young believers have earnestly prayed for it. However, the anointing does not walk into you, you must walk by faith into it.

God must be promoted to the number one priority if apostolic anointing is to reach a person's heart. God must rise. The key to revival and growth is straightforward: God must rise. God can only rise when we recognize the only truth that matters, God rises by an absolute revelation of the power of Jesus Christ.

Jesus said, "I am the door. No one can approach the father except through me."

Jesus Christ must be returned to the center of everything we do. Churches must again serve God and the Kingdom with fervency and passion. Programs have their place, but they cannot distract from a relationship with Jesus. Personal feelings, leadership personalities, and other humanistic stratagems must be considered, but Jesus must be placed at the forefront of everything.

The key that unlocks the door is the attitude of reverence with which we approach the King. The door is the power and authority of the Master that in turn envelops the true believer. One is not complete without the other. We must walk in the humility of Christ to possess the apostolic nature of Christ. We must possess the key to step through the door to the fulfillment of end-time prophecy concerning God's church.

Prisons With Stained Glass Windows

4
LOVE IS THE MOVEMENT

The modernization of religion has redefined the concept of love. The charismatic movement ushered in a renewal of compassion. The concept of personally connecting to people has replaced attempts to merely convert others to doctrine. Catch phrases such as, "People don't care how much you know until they know how much you care," have become the prominent mantra of this evangelistic era.

In attempts to reach the un-churched, many Christians have tried small groups that meet in homes as a replacement for the midweek service. Door prizes and giveaways are another popular trend to attract others to worship events. Instead of traditional door knocking, church planters have placed more emphasis on programs that benefit the community. Many mega churches have separate bank accounts to specifically target the homeless, orphans, and widows. More multicultural congregations are being established, as Spanish daughter works are born in every part of the country. It would seem that these are all positive indicators of the church's standing with God. After all, Jesus taught many of these principles as He walked the earth.

However, if we are not careful power will decrease as numbers increase. More people with serious issues attend our services, but less are transformed and delivered. The world bring sin, lustful attitudes, gossiping spirits, destructive methods, and selfish agendas into the church. Often, the church isn't equipped to handle it, because "love," as we know it, is not enough to withstand the onslaught of satanic attack.

> **A church sets itself up for failure anytime it prepares for revival but does not pray for it.**

The enemy is a master manipulator. He recklessly assaults the church's weaknesses. In this case, he uses the church's "love" against it. As the church has shifted its attention to others instead of God, it has lost sensitivity, vision, and power. The enemy doesn't care if we grow outwardly focused. What he fears most is balance. The church terrifies Satan when it sells out to the King and engages in the Kingdom.

A church sets itself up for failure any time it prepares for revival but does not pray for it. It sets up for pain when it programs for revival but does not spiritually progress. It will disintegrate when it naturally postures for revival without providing a foundation of spiritual preparedness. The definition of an unbalanced church is one in which natural growth extends beyond the level of spiritual maturity, or one in which "spiritual maturity" causes a lapse in natural progression. Many churches that started with integrity, righteousness, holiness, and apostolic authority have been reduced to nothing a short time later. Growth occurred. People came. God even moved. Why the tragic end?

In its formative stages, the church is usually full of people sold out to its vision. Its members establish themselves in the Kingdom and desire to do more for God. Holiness is not minimized. Rather, believers view it as one of the focal points of serving God. Prayer and fasting are not optional. They are the basis of the church's functioning. That's when the church begins to grow, and that rapid growth is often where the journey away from apostolic anointing begins.

As the church develops, new converts present different ideas. Through time, newer leaders replace older ones. The newer leaders have more modern views. This usually translates to less holiness and spiritual mindedness, because many newer leaders are given influence before adequately being established in doctrine. If the wisdom and spiritual development of the church are not staying ahead of the worldliness coming in, true balance cannot be maintained. If this occurs, confusion results. The gradual shift is inward and downward, for the natural shift of humanity is never toward God. Therefore, a truly apostolic church not only programs for reaching toward the world, but it is also innovative in turning its people toward God.

UNRESTRAINED

It is impossible for a human to reach a place of unconditional love without the prevailing power of God. In vain attempts to become Christ-like, the church makes decisions that ultimately lead to its demise. We cannot just develop a mentality under the guise of love that is completely tolerate and permissive. Love without demands offers no chance for loyalty. Love without restrictions offers no chance for trust. Men, who mistakenly believed they could emulate God's love by becoming more tolerant of people's sins, conceptualized restriction-less love. Tolerance does allow mercy and grace to flow more freely, but it does not preclude the fact that judgment is delayed but not denied. Therefore, to ignore sin in order to demonstrate God's love only exhibits man's arrogance.

Man cannot play God. Therefore, although the church grants reprieve under the guise of toleration, the long-term effects of sin and ungodliness are staggering to both the new believer and the church. From the onset, the new convert fails to learn and learns how to fail. Instead of the church teaching that failure and struggle are a necessary part of life, it often casts a blind eye toward these struggles and failures altogether. By neither confirming nor confronting, feathers are not ruffled, but we do not insure a new believer's growth, maturation, or stabilization either. A spirit of complete toleration could destroy the sheer essence and purity of the church.

God is love. However, God does place demands on humanity. Unbridled power is unhealthy and dangerous.

Passion is a potent tool, yet unbridled passion destroys. Position without discipline is dangerous. Love without restraint is just as debilitating. The great paradox of God's love is that although it is unconditional, it is still not unrestrained. The two are not the same.

The modern church has created a convergence of these two beliefs that has led to a weakening of apostolic power by minimizing the importance of repentance. Repentance is rarely taught in many congregations, except to non-church members who are attempting to receive the Holy Ghost. To admit a need for repentance among the membership is like admitting failure. To divulge this is to deny perfection by embracing fallen humanity. This lack of self-examination makes it easy for the flesh to remain hidden behind actions extending into drab places, for pale shades appear as light in the darkness. The church cannot ignore the darkness within. We are still human, so by necessity, love must establish boundaries.

Love is not unsympathetic. It's not judgmental, hypocritically looking down at others. However, neither is it blindly forbearing. In order for true love to exist, it must be reciprocated. Any relationship in which one party gives while the other only takes is not healthy. God's love demanded that He sacrifice for us. How can we require any less of ourselves?

HISTORICAL PERSPECTIVE

Most young leaders currently piloting the apostolic movement face two pertinent questions. What do I do with a heritage that was hard? Is it worth compromising a few details to get results (does the end justify the means)?

Today's young leaders are appalled at the pattern of aggressive "love." Judgmental attitudes predominant in many circles hinder church growth and apostolic authority. The few churches still operating under that mentality are small, barren, and lifeless. This is not the example that younger and more educated (not wiser) leaders wish to follow. Also, after witnessing many new Christians being spiritually murdered for not upholding the standards of the church, the next generation shifted into an era of acceptance. However, the danger of transition is the risk of overcompensation. One does not right the car dangerously careening off the road by yanking the wheel in the opposite direction. One ditch is no better than the other. Some things need to be corrected, but over-correction is just as deadly as not correcting at all. The great tragedy of this generation is the tendency to do the wrong things with the right motivation. Although the motive may be pure, it stifles spiritual progress. Everyone agrees that impure motives cause immediate damage. However, blind ambition obliterates just as swiftly.

THE CURSE OF TALENT

Many of today's brightest and most gifted leaders fall victim to the snare of narcissism. The tendency of talent is always inward. The moment man establishes control of his own life, God steps out. The curse of talented people is the tendency to lose focus on God and look first toward selfish desires.

Even the most unlearned leaders understand the rules. There are political and social mores that must be followed if the ladder is to be climbed. Refuse those traditions, and the descent will be quicker than the rise. Therefore, most play within the unspoken but clearly established boundaries.

We do and say the right things. We do that even with motives to elevate status. God opens few doors today, because men have forced so many open on their own that He no longer has room to operate. A believer loses perspective, the moment he chooses flesh over God. A carnal, selfish perspective is one of the greatest setbacks to personal anointing.

Individual motives must be continually evaluated. Failure to examine every thought leads to personal crisis. It is easier to control one's actions than one's mind. So many young people stray because of this. They continually attempt to do and forever forget to be, becoming so intoxicated with doing the works of Christianity that they forget to truly become a Christian.

AVERAGE EXCELLENCE

Excellence is one of the foundational disciplines of Scriptural theology. Peter instructed the church to adjoin excellence and Christian faith as the foundation of every other discipline. As leadership knowledge and team theories have exponentially increased over the last couple of decades, the church has paid much attention to the virtue of excellence, encouraging it in every part of a Christian's life.

However, the gravest danger is to ignorantly live in a state of average excellence, attempting to do everything right only as it appears in the natural. Talent has become an intense focus within the church. Advancements in technology and media have profoundly added to the rise of external excellence. These upgrades to traditional church services are ways of increasing visual aesthetics. Multimodal services are one reason many congregations see a significant increase in attendance. People no longer feel the dry effects of religion. Instead, they find entertainment value in the church. While the church has never been a source of amusement, it is in constant competition with other avenues that seek man's attention. Therefore, the church has adapted to meet current cultural demands. Failure to appeal to people on the level of their current value system is a mistake. Blindly trusting old methods to capture the entire gamete of human emotion no longer works. The church needs to modernize its methodology, and many churches are doing just that.

The resistance to such change by some churches is directly correlated to the overreaction of many prominent leaders. Not only have some church's traded anointing for entertainment value, but in an attempt to modernize and rid itself of yesterday's dirty laundry (judgmental attitudes), they have not only looked for modern methods, but also a modern message. The dilemma is that the methods are changeable, but the message is non-compromising and nonnegotiable. It is unapologetic. Truth always transcends culture.

Average excellence is the result of either offense. Failure to modify methods to influence the

> **The very nature of God is offensive to the flesh.**

larger segments of an advanced society produces limited results. There are two sides to the "live for God" coin, the natural and the spiritual. Spiritual excellence, without the benefit of natural excellence, produces few moments of progressive significance. However, the opposite is also true. Modifying the message in an attempt to reach more people with an "un-offensive gospel" is neither compelling nor functional.

The very temperament of the doctrine is distasteful to the unbeliever. The very nature of God is offensive to the flesh. While many would brazenly declare this is sacrilege, it is true that humanity rebels against the nature of God. Man's depravity prevents him from desiring a spiritual way of life. To send a message that is not challenging is an embarrassment. The very power of conviction is being systematically removed for fear of being controversial. However, what the world needs is a church that will remain impenitent in truth. The world needs a church that will allow conviction to reign.

THE GUISE OF LOVE

True love is always concerned with the greater good. It doesn't exist for the singularity of the moment. However, this generation operates under an assumption that love minimizes today's sins to ensure tomorrow's sanctity. This mentality is neither Biblical nor Godly. However, at its core, the doctrine of toleration presents this concept. Total toleration theory pushes an idea that there is nothing sacred if one is attempting to save a soul. Reaching lost humanity is of utmost importance and should be undertaken by any means possible. Doctrine is not to be deified and is secondary to the purpose of the church, which is to reach for sinners. The methods aimed at maximizing this potential have moved from a God focus to humanitarian efforts. The methods employed are not anti-Biblical and seem acceptable on the surface level. For instance, the church has long needed to engage the widows, homeless, fatherless, and poor. However, any truth that calls for less consecration in order to create revival is not from God, no matter how cleverly crafted or whose voice it has behind it.

God has never demanded less and given more. Any move of significant spiritual consequence has always been preceded by repentance, separation from the world, prayer, fasting, and renewed consecration. That formula has never changed and cannot be diluted with the expectation of more powerful results. When man feels the need to change the message in order to improve effectiveness, it is never a sign that the message no longer performs. It is a clear indicator that the man is no longer connected to the power behind the message, for God's power needs no gimmicks.

Love masks itself the moment it dispels old truths to bring new results. Confusion results because some have had notable success abandoning moral and doctrinal theology. Every minister who walks away from God's Word is not destined to become a natural failure. This assumption is what drives many conservative Christians crazy and causes many borderline conservative Christians to take the plunge of removing their ties to the doctrine.

The church must realize that in the natural (which is where we live); charisma, excitement, passion, and personality can create momentum. A man can build a church on these elements alone in some cases. However, the potential lid for that church is substantially lowered due to limited leadership perspective. Jesus told Peter that to live by the sword means he would also die by the sword. The same natural principles that seem to free the church from doctrinal "tyranny" are the same principles that lead to weakness, loss of purpose, confusion, and limited apostolic authority.

Lost in the melodrama of humanitarian Christianity alone is the blind eye it casts toward sin. Toleration demands that limited reprimand be placed on the guilty. Mercy and grace operate in a clandestine manner, concealing matters of eternal consequence. For someone just beginning the journey toward God, this approach may appear compelling. However, the dilemma is that tolerance is not just given to a few. It reaches outward, making it easier for church leaders and ministers to sin by removing their responsibility for actions taken.

How can that statement be true? Examine the instances of many churches that followed leaders down the road of toleration doctrines. They brought people to church. God responded to the needs and the hunger present. Problems developed involving holiness doctrinal views. Wrong decisions were made because it's always easier to back up than it is to move forward. Standards were lowered to make people feel more comfortable. However, the effect of lowering standards to reach people cannot be contained to new converts, for it will inevitably seep into the hearts of the less committed original members. One decision to remove a holiness concept leads to another, and soon new outreach programs are started that bring even less value to traditional beliefs. This creates a spiraling effect. Once the church has opened the door toward less consecration, it is almost impossible to close. These cycles usually end with both the church and its leaders spiraling out of control, coldly denouncing doctrines once held sacred. This whole scenario unfolds under the guise of a Godly love for fellowman. It's the absolute danger of ultimate toleration, the church is fooled into losing its power in earnest attempts to serve God's purpose. That is why purpose that is not firmly rooted in God's word is completely dangerous.

ACCOUNTABILITY

The world has set up a culture where most want personal demands to be met but few live up to the demands of others. In short, responsibility and accountability are ancient relics of apostolic authority. Many current positional leaders expect respect and obedience without paying the price to earn it. Instead, they depend on position to create reverence.

However, position has corrupted as many potential leaders as it's produced. Power, without accountability, leads to failure, for it naturally corrupts human will. The predictable shift is always inward. For this reason, accountability among leaders is a must. Total toleration demands that accountability be removed, and that is what exposes and weakens this flawed belief system. Culture has made it far too easy for Christians to live in ways that do not please God. This has a trickle down effect and will ultimately lead to the weakening of the church as a whole. We must not allow that trend to continue.

CONCLUSION

An enormous paradox is that a world supposedly ruled by love, still introduces such grave issues of hate. Increased humanitarian efforts have not been able to stop the masses from starving. Countless wells are not slowing the rate of the world's thirst and starvation. Christian portrayal and proclamation of love has not decreased the propaganda of hate spreading across the globe like a disease. Children are still molested at increasingly frightening rates. Homes are ravaged by divorce on astronomical levels. Statistics comparing the alcohol consumption, pornography viewing, and illicit affairs of Christians to their non-Christian counterparts shows an almost equal dispersion. These numbers indicate that while the church desperately attempts to address people's natural needs, it is not meeting spiritual needs. Even when church is attended, there's little apostolic power present to change lives. The church must face the reality that shifting cultural trends may dictate a schematic change but never a doctrinal one.

On the other hand, doctrine must not be deified. Jesus insisted that He was the Truth. Therefore, the message of holiness standards is just doctrine. It is possible to live the message and never know the Truth. Living principle outside of relationship is just as destructive as leading by position with no regulation. Love demands that there be balance, and those demands must be met, for love is the movement of God's culture.

5
THE DEVIL IS IN THE DETAILS

Modern evangelical methodology has dramatically shifted concerning evangelism over the past decade. This shift has caused a significant fracture in the fundamental formula of apostolic living. It is entirely possible under current trends to mass produce revivals and call them successful without ever establishing real change in people's lives. Attendance records, baptismal numbers, and how many received God's Spirit determine success by evangelistic terms. Ignored is the fact that a few weeks after the "revival," most churches return to business as usual. The retention rate of people who passed through the doors is usually minimal.

Some progressive evangelists tout themselves as modern day revivalists by providing evidence that their methods result in large crowds. They guarantee that they'll have the church packed on Sunday morning. Under these plans, the church works the community with giveaways and food, all building toward a massive Sunday service that is focused on bringing the community into the church. For the most part, these methods work, and many churches like the results. The concern is that this fad is another microwave sensation that quickly produces results that will not last. However, we observe the initial numbers, failing to recognize that mass production without quality control is wrong. Evangelism without discipleship is not only foolish, it is dangerous.

It is alarming how many people pass through the doors who never get a real opportunity to grow. Most churches are simply not equipped to handle a quick influx of new people. There is minimal time for one-on-one instruction, building relationships, or establishing rapport. These limitations cause the church to lose contact information, making follow-up after the momentous event almost impossible. The same evidence that proves the "success" of modern evangelistic endeavors also indicates that the proverbial back door is wide open. The retention rate of these first-time guests who pack the church on this one memorable Sunday is remarkably low. In many cases, there are a large number of people who are baptized and filled with the Holy Ghost. However, far too many leave that service to never be seen again. The numbers in this case are an anomaly, in that they present only one side of the equation. Current evangelists book their schedules full, while the church ignores true long-term impact (or lack thereof). We must seek God about gaining better influence than a megaservice. Positive statistics are of little Kingdom significance if the people return to their sins. We must stop fixating on the value of numbers and focus on the value of souls. The responsibility is not on the evangelists who employ such methods, it is on the church to close the back door. These powerful methods that attract large numbers are great first impressions, but the church must be responsible for maintaining the momentum that the evangelist has generated. We just get better at keeping those that God saves in our churches.

NO SHORTCUTS

The greatest danger of modern evangelism is that it has caused a loss of patience, an attribute that has preceded every significant move of God. Jesus told the early church to wait until He gave them power. There was no indication how long they would have to wait. They simply went to Jerusalem, started a prayer meeting, and remained until God showed up. Ignoring this process has always been detrimental to the Kingdom.

The Bible states that God commits to a process for saving people. Scripture also instructs that we are to run with "patience" and "wait" upon the Lord. The fastest runner doesn't win the race in the spiritual arena. The emotionally strong attain spiritual victory. Scripture demands an obvious expectation toward growth. Babies are to drink the sincere milk, but there comes a time when the bottle has to be removed, and meat must be added to the diet. According to Peter, a Christian begins with basic faith but must complete a journey that ends in Christ-like love. Paul encouraged Christians to forget the things behind them and fight to advance toward the destination before them. From Old to New Testament, the Bible indicates that the Kingdom of God is neither stationary nor hastily established.

Abraham infamously bypassed God's plan to pursue a quicker arrangement. The world still suffers from the greatest shortcut blunder in history. Nations clash and hatred remains from the two cultures that diverged from a sidestep mentality. The miracle had already been promised. A divine plan had already been set in motion. This agreement from God included a ready-made miracle for a couple that was well past their fertile years. However, Abraham grew weary in waiting. He looked at a younger version of his wife and decided that God needed help to bring about this impossibility. Big mistake.

This lesson is evident even in the nature of new converts. In teaching Bible studies in the past, I observed an extremely intriguing trend. Usually the people that I worked the least to bring to the fullness of truth lasted the least amount of time. However, these people create the most excitement among the church. I would teach an hour Bible study. They would pray, receive the Holy Ghost, and desire to be baptized all in the same night. The revelation of the Scriptures leapt of the pages and engrossed them, plainly illuminating the darkness. The Spirit moved. The church rejoiced. All was well with the world.

The problem is that almost without exception, these people who quickly grasped the truth, would just as quickly un-grasp it when a leader from their own faith rebutted the teaching. There was no bond that tightly gripped them, keeping the truth stable and secure in their hearts and minds.

However, the reverse also proved to be true. There were people that had to be taught and re-taught multiple times with no sign of change. They stayed interested in the subject but almost seemed to continue dialogue solely to refute what I was trying to present. The world didn't seem so congenial. There was remarkably little rejoicing. Honestly, fleshly thoughts of why should I continue to waste my time when there were people who were obviously more "hungry" and accepting lingered. However, I learned that persistence, kindness, and patience, pay off. These same people often turned the corner, and unlike the others, they never looked back. There is something to be said for those who stick with the process and remain patient regardless of the outlook. We must learn to rid ourselves of a shortcut mentality.

DISCIPLES

We're living in a culture that no longer devotes to discipleship. In this hour, it's easy to be in church. It is a lot less likely that the church be in us. We're often found possessing Christ, but we're far less likely to be possessed by Him. The church is full of participants but short on disciples.

One cannot be a disciple without discipline. By its sheer nature, discipline takes time to be established. The church is full of people engrossed in the benefits and blessings of Christendom but uninterested in the obedience and restraint required to live a crucified life. The problem is that as this attitude implants itself into church culture, new converts develop this same outlook.

> **The church is full of participants but short on disciples.**

It's easy to fall victim to the fallacy that the more "churchy" the church becomes in its approach, the harder it is to be an effective witness in the world. This is manifested in one of two ways under contemporary church culture. First of all, many mainstream believers are severing all forms of physical identification toward truth. Compromising outward holiness because some unkind people turned others off with their egotistical attitudes is foolish. Just because extremists over-concentrated the formula does not mean that the formula must now be diluted. Truth cannot be oversimplified because others made it too complicated. It is forever settled.

When a church removes itself from sanctification and holiness in order to attract people, it backs away from the apostolic covering that has made it powerful. Obedience and submission remain the hallmarks of apostolic anointing. Any entity that removes itself from that divine order does so with misguided expectations. Charisma, talent, kindness, and exceptional programs will lead to natural success and numerical growth under mainstream guidelines. However, real change of everlasting consequence cannot thrive where natural order rules. Natural order subverts eternal principles and causes an upheaval in the supernatural arena. Questioning from a heart of impure motives always leads to compromise, and compromise always leads to spiritual weakness. Belief without substance is empty. One cannot claim to possess the substance of Christ while forgetting His principles, even if they do so under the guise of religious tolerance.

The second manifestation of this problem is the exact opposite. There are those so hardcore in protecting values that they do so at the expense of new people. There is no greater threat to the growth of the Kingdom than people who have the right beliefs but undermine those beliefs because of arrogant attitudes or misguided notions of loyalty. It is one thing to defend the doctrine. It is entirely different to "protect" the doctrine against anyone who fails to understand or disagrees for lack of revelation.

Often, self-proclaiming protectors of holiness are nothing more than doctrinal deity worshippers. Despite the fact that the Bible says the letter of the law kills, many still make it their life, ridiculing and belittling the rest of the world. Emotions prosper, cultivated in unstable hearts like a highly explosive compound in a volatile container. In the haze of self-exaltation, the church has lost the compassion, patience, and love of Christ. Men become demigods, because they feel that their beliefs add to their existence instead of recognizing that God is the only thing that truly adds value. Belief without substance is empty, and one cannot claim to possess the substance of Christ while tearing down others, even if they do so under the guise of spiritual warfare.

> **A carnal attitude protecting a spiritual principle is one of the most damning aspects of Christianity.**

A common misconception leading to intolerance is the belief that people immediately become a new creature when filled with the Holy Ghost. The Bible does state that we become new creatures. However, the literal understanding of that statement is out of context. The Word of God was not advocating that people would be immediately changed into His image and never sin immediately after being filled with the Holy Ghost. Instantly their disposition, attitude, performance, appearance, and personality change, and they become a "real" child of God. The journey from initiation to completion is instantaneous. This is honestly how many believers view their conversion, but it's not what the Bible teaches.

The facts are far removed from that fantastical fixation. The Holy Ghost leads to all truth (John 16:13). There is a process of learning that must take place. Once a new convert receives the Holy Ghost, he is not converted to a doctrine. He's converted to a relationship that empowers him to grasp principles of eternal consequence. The blinders come off, and for the first time, a sinner sees life for what it is.

The reality is that sin may still occur at this point, for humanity has not ceased to exist. Many born again believers have become so distanced from sin that they have forgotten what it means to be a degenerate sinner. We have lived under the liberty of the Holy Ghost for so long that we fail to grasp that freedom is not free. Christ purchased it with His own blood and sacrifice. We also fail to remember that true freedom is not the right to do wrong. True freedom gives us the right to do right. Under the natural order of humanity, man had no power over the stronghold of sin. However, the freedom that Christ purchased at Calvary usurped the power of man's transgressions. The moment a person receives God's Spirit in their life, they are no longer held hostage by hell, no longer bound by a mindset that magnifies human frailty and imperfections. They are indeed transformed into a new creature, a new creature that has the capability to learn the ways of God while unlearning the ways of man.

It is impossible for man to come to significant revelation outside of God's presence. Paul's letter to Timothy discusses many evil and carnal acts that oppose and influence modern believers (II Timothy 3). He indicated that men would be knowledge seekers. However, despite the fact that they would be intellectual, they would also be self-centered. This is a deadly combination, for self-centeredness and knowledge usually lead to self-deception. Any time God stops speaking but man keeps receiving revelation, there is a colossal problem. The Scripture refers to this as people who are always learning but never coming to knowledge of the truth (II Timothy 3:7). It is entirely possible to learn the principles and concepts of Christianity and miss the Christ at its center. It is also possible to misunderstand that new converts need time to adapt and adjust to the new climate they find themselves in.

Paul, again in a letter to Timothy, differentiated between the idea of salvation and knowledge of truth (1 Timothy 2:3-4). He stated that God wanted all men to be saved, and to come to the knowledge of the truth. Salvation does not relate to an immediate transfer in the arena of revelation. His statement gives the inclination that salvation is the precursor to a deeper knowledge that leads to greater relationship.

The book of Corinthians reveals that the natural man cannot understand the things of the Spirit (1 Corinthians 2:14). Trying to understand spiritual principles from a carnal mindset will never work. That is why so many people cannot grasp the sacrifice and commitment of the apostolic movements greatest proponents. Most peer into a spiritual window only through fleshly eyes. They aren't prompted to view sacrifice and commitment the way the spiritually minded do.

Every indication suggests that the Holy Ghost is not the immediate transformer that alters people into angelic form right after conversion. Scripture indicates that we receive the Spirit of God so that we could have the opportunity to receive instruction and knowledge about God and His goodness toward us (1 Corinthians 2:12).

This should lead to an immediate change in the way many treat new converts. The Holy Ghost should be allowed time to work. A person is not hopeless because they received the Holy Ghost one day and did not change every immature and inappropriate behavior immediately. There are many things a new convert will learn to change. The church must learn to be patient with this process. Many new people are stunted in their development because a misguided few with positive intentions make negative impacts. Many times, discouragement from church people can lead to a lack of production and growth. At times, the enemy does not have to distract a new convert. His job is expertly done for him. If not careful, those within the church could weaken and overwhelm the very person it has sworn to defend and nurture.

Paul lived on the forefront of evangelistic focus by ensuring that his compassion for lost souls would never be extinguished. He lived with the constant awareness that regardless of the good he was doing in the world, at his core, he was still the lowest of sinners. This perspective does not allow one to look down at others with judgmental stares and a conceited heart. One cannot view his fellow man harshly while knowing that there would be condemnation and rejection in his own life except for grace. It's hard to judge others when one remembers that without the power of God and the mercy that He bestowed, you would be nothing.

Many feel entitled because we have grown up in the glory of God's presence. We have seen and felt Him working in the immediate past. We've grown accustomed to His holiness. If we aren't careful, this causes us to feel cleansed, and we forget that our righteousness is as filthy rags in His eyes. We aren't good enough without Christ. Therefore, we cannot and should not judge others. Marred vision will always find fault and flaws, for broken reflections are all we can see without the clarity of the Spirit guiding us.

AVERAGE EXCELLENCE REVISITED

The value of excellence is highly discussed today. Leadership development, ministry training, business education, and athletic motivation all discuss taking pride in the quality of work. The church should approach the Kingdom of God and winning the lost with the same level of distinction.

The church appeals to people on two levels. There is a natural appeal, and there is a spiritual appeal. Failure in either area can be detrimental to the level of attraction that a church has on a prospective convert. Many people walk away from the truth (doctrine) before they ever experience the Truth (God). Most often, this is because they subconsciously rejected the natural appeal of the church they were attending, or they never connected with the spirit of the church.

In his book, *10 Rules of Youth Ministry and Why 180 Breaks Them All*, Blaine Bartel details how much attention man pays to natural detail. He mentions that the Bible states that Man observes the outward appearance while God observes the heart (1 Samuel 16:7). Most often, we only consider this verse from God's perspective. Man may be fooled by outward appearances of perfection, but God knows the thoughts and intents of our hearts. While this interpretation is not theologically inaccurate, Bartel suggests that there is another principle that is missed. He proposes that God was also revealing a principle for the church to use in attracting people to the Kingdom of God. Men are attracted by what they see and feel. Bartel intimates that we should use that advantage and become as naturally attractive as possible without risking spiritual depth.

This is not a novel idea. Most preachers and scholars of the early church used these principles. Jesus even used the benefit of being relevant by means of parables. Many of history's most noted Biblical scholars, teachers, and preachers have become adept at the use of language, storytelling, humor, anecdotes, proverbs, poems, physical demonstrations, and many other details to aesthetically appeal to their listeners. Only the foolish argue that it is wrong to connect with people on a human level. There is never a problem with trying to reach people where they live. Human rules, concepts, emotions, and thoughts can all be stimulated on the base level of human interaction.

The entertainment industry figured this out long ago. Mainstream artists and entertainers from every genre fight to reign in the areas of talent and performance. Many of the brightest stars today not only promote themselves by selling their abilities, they also pay millions for producers to design the best stage and present the best visual and auditory array.

People want to forget reality, if only for a few moments. This is life in the 21st century. The church must be aware and tap into the mainstream ideas of society. Pre-modern views were great from the standpoint of yesterday when people's senses were not bombarded with multimodal information every day. If new life is to become attracted to our churches, it cannot happen by simply convincing young people that they do not need to be engrossed in culture. It will happen by creating a subculture that offers God in ways the world is looking.

God is not afraid of new methods. He never has been. Study the Scripture and one will find that God was always bringing new works and wonders to the eyes of Israel. Newness has never been a problem for Him. It is time for the church to create an image that matches current culture without devaluing apostolic convictions. We must find a way to achieve that balance.

There is nothing wrong with a church that demands excellence in its music program. I wish we could scream that from the rooftops and let its truth resound in the ears of every church across America. I remember the days when we could sing old hymns from worn out songbooks while someone who could barely sing led the choir. Then, people would respond. I haven't forgotten the many services when God's Spirit swept across an assembly, and people cried and received the Holy Ghost while someone pounded an untuned piano and sang off key. I'm not naive enough to believe that God no longer moves in those types of services. God doesn't need man's talent or excellence to produce supernatural outpourings. He never has.

However, the point has never been whether or not God needs natural excellence to operate. The point is how ineffective natural ineptness is at reaching the majority of people who have grown up under current societal views. The answer is staggering and extremely alarming. It is not effective at all. Most churches that view change as a threat are rooted in a vicious cycle that leads to minimal growth. Most have little impact on their communities, yet are satisfied because "worldly principles are not indoctrinating their churches." To clarify, that is not to say that all smaller churches suffer from this mentality. I was raised in a small church and give all the credit in the world to the faithful pastors who lead them.

The truth is that a church should be attractive to people on a natural level. The worship service should be attractive on the level of talent. The musicians should be able to play the songs. The ministry should strive to speak plainly. The yard should be kept up. The building should be clean. The bathrooms should be presentable. The church body should be warm, friendly, and inviting. People should be able to see the love of God by viewing the disposition of the believers. Teachers at all levels should be well prepared and not just throw a few thoughts together before they get to church. There should be some long-term objective, something they build toward. Children should be attracted to the Sunday School Department and find relevant and fun material in the classrooms. Teenagers should find the youth group exciting and full of activities that challenge them to be different from the world while providing an outlet for the separation being encouraged. Parents should be excited about the family atmosphere and friendly environment. There are no excuses for a church that is not trying to reach the maximum amount of people possible. If that is the mission, it takes excellence.

Some will oppose this concept. However, it does not change the fact that many people who could be reached are not moved toward our churches because they feel that we have little to offer them. We have the greatest gift in the world. However, they'll never see it because they cannot look past the bad image of ourselves that we present. It's a shame for others to blinded to God because I'm standing in the way. It's also a sin.

Arrogance isn't the only manifestation of pride that will keep many from being saved. Unwillingness to change while we watch the world fall around us is not only sad, it is irresponsible. Many people claim that yesterday's commitment to spiritual excellence is all that's needed to grow a church in today's world. However, excellence that is only demonstrated spiritually is unbalanced. It is not attractive to those who are not spiritually minded (the ones we're trying to reach). This imbalance may make for a strong church body, but it provides little support for growth and development of new people. We must become relevant to people who are in desperate need of a Savior. We must find a way to engage the world without sacrificing morals. We can find that way through the guidance of the Holy Ghost. Excellence that is only spiritual in nature is only an average excellence.

Hopefully, you are still with me at this point because, as Bishop T.F. Tenney has said on several occasions, "There are two sides to every pancake." In an attempt to relate to culture and grow churches more quickly, some leaders have almost totally abandoned spiritual principles to strengthen natural appeal. This is not only ludicrous, it undermines the apostolic nature that gives a church the dimension needed to change lives. Emotional attraction without the underlying drawing of God in man's heart is dangerous. It leaves people asking a question that shouldn't be asked of an apostolic church.

"I am entertained, but where is the power?"

Music is a powerful weapon in the arsenal of those who know how to use it. Add the dimension and depth of exceptionally talented musicians, and one has the perfect ingredients for an awesome service. Dynamic shifts in music can bring people to tears, applause, or dance. If we aren't careful, the powerful pull that music has on heartstrings can lead to emotionalism and sensationalism, diverting us from true worship.

In the modern evangelical experience, it is possible for a sinner to leave a church service unchanged, yet still feel as if a life altering encounter has occurred. It is possible to leave having "worshipped God" and stirred emotions without ever tipping the iceberg of God's existence. God desires so much more from the apostolic church than tickled sensations. He longs for services that offer the miraculous and transform lives.

Singers and musicians who practice but rarely pray open the door to self-intoxication. Being a vessel of the anointing, on any level, is a privilege, not a right. Power only comes through connection to God, and that connection only comes through prayer. If a church is going to be powerfully apostolic, those who lead must be people of passion and prayer. There are no exceptions.

I have heard preachers and musicians debate which group is more needed in today's church. Music attracts people more than preaching; therefore, music must be more beneficial. Others say music cannot save. The spoken Word of God saves men. None of the people that founded the church were musicians. They were preachers. Therefore, preaching is more valuable. Both arguments are erroneous. God needs neither, yet He chooses and supports both. He fully expects His church to do the same. We are supposed to be laborers together, working hand-in-hand for the Kingdom of God.

My sister-in-law, Jennifer Pavlu, has developed into a tremendous worship leader over the past several years. Her commitment to detail and excellence is highly noted in every service. Both she, and her husband Jared, work tirelessly to make sure that everything is in order before the service. Their behind the scenes labor and prayer ensure that balance is achieved. Like many worship leaders, she gives everything she has in a worship service. However, what sets her apart from many is that after she walks off the platform, her passion for the Kingdom doesn't stop there. She supports the preacher with the same tenacity with which she attacks the worship service. She prays for people in the altars as often as she can, looking for more ways to be a blessing than just through a song. She doesn't just live, breathe, and sleep music… She lives, breathes, and sleeps the Kingdom, and that is what makes her ministry so anointed. It's not about her. It's about bringing God glory, exalting Him, and inspiring others to do the same.

This is the attitude of someone with a Kingdom mindset, someone who knows the importance of the relationship between preaching and music. This is the commitment and attitude that God desires all leaders to possess.

We are in this fight together, working to create an atmosphere that crescendos into apostolic anointing. That cannot effectively happen if the platform and pulpit are divided.

Those involved in preaching God's Word should be prayerful enough to know the voice of God. It's not enough to only preach the words of other talented ministers from religious society. It's not enough to bring a word from a book, Internet, or compact disk. The church is in desperate need of a rhema word from God, a fresh word that melts hearts, builds faith, challenges sin, reinforces convictions, and renews relationship with God. The world again waits for the manifestation of the sons of God, people who will be sensitive to the operation of the Spirit (Romans 8:19).

Love needs to emanate from every believer. Every guest should feel kindness and compassion rising from a service that's full of Godly conviction. Grace must be extended, especially when someone seems unworthy of it. Submission to leadership and pastoral authority must again be demonstrated, for this is the only highway down which the supernatural flows. Mediocre service can no longer be tolerated. We must find a personal altar and consecrate to God.

We cannot expect programs to build the church. They are effective tools and are much needed. However, programs alone will never create an apostolic revival. If not properly balanced, programs take attention from prayer, fasting, and study of God's Word. Programs may rob us of seeking and sacrificing until we find God. We have found that it is possible to have good church with music, media, and methodology. However, if we lack prayer, we're proceeding without the power source of the apostolic movement. Prayer is vital to the survival of the apostolic church.

We urgently need an overwhelming feeling of impending judgment to awaken us from slumber. The writer of Corinthians said, "Knowing therefore the terror of the Lord, we persuade men," (2 Corinthians 5:11). An understanding that many die and face eternity without God everyday should provoke us to the point of action. We must become men and women of prayer, if we're going to reach the world for Christ.

Fasting has to be more than a fad if we're going to pound the flesh into submission. We must understand that the true purpose of fasting was never to gain or accomplish anything in the natural. The purpose of fasting is to kill the flesh, to weaken its stronghold.

Often natural results occur, but this is more a byproduct of the flesh being hindered than God granting a wish. If we returned to the commitment of the early church toward prayer and fasting, we would be more effective witnesses for Christ. Removed would be the nervousness that discounts so many believers. Miracles would once again take place on our streets. The enemy would once again fear believers. God wants the church to return to supernatural ministry, and we must strive for it. However, excellence that is only natural is only average excellence.

CONCLUSION

As individuals, we must examine the influence we truly possess. If we were honest, most would discover that our influence is remarkably small. We spend most of our time working to win a few close friends or family members to God, if we are doing that. Many Christians simply stay in the confines of already saved friends and family, while wondering why their impact on the Kingdom is minimal. We must expand our horizons and become comfortable outside the bubble of our own existence. We must be willing to walk into uncharted waters to advance the cause that is Christ.

We live as though we fully trust the programs of the church to reach the world. We must understand that God does back strong programs and utilize human talent to accomplish His purpose. He does demand natural excellence to be ingrained into every fiber of His church body. He is also serious about spiritual excellence. God is not interested in tipping the scales in either direction. He desires for His church to find true balance.

True balance insists that we attract people in their own element. We must appeal to man in the area of the five senses. However, we understand that this approach only goes so far. True change occurs at the level of God's Spirit. We need greater anointing and spiritual sensitivity. However, spiritual revelation stops being received when natural interest is lost. We need a deeper connection between the two. The devil is in the details, and his plan is brilliant. He either wants the church to be so "spiritual" that it loses all natural attraction or so naturally superior that it loses all apostolic authority. God designed a church that flows on both levels, and He expects the modern church to meet His expectations.

Prisons With Stained Glass Windows

6
THE MARKETPLACE

As a Christian nation, liberalism and humanism have dramatically drawn the masses, wreaking havoc in the natural world. Statistics on cultural trends are insignificant, because the world has climatically changed, setting the stage for the return of Christ. This shift has been progressing over the past few decades, exploding into the chaotic and confusing conundrum of today. The current spiritual temperature of America is alarming. Spirituality is becoming more and more about personal experiences with nature or diverse self-awakenings that make the individual his or her own god. Movements that people would have scoffed at a few years ago are taken seriously by some of the world's most influential people. Scientology, the belief that we are aliens trapped in human bodies, has become a current fad. On this journey, one discovers more and more about their inner nature, until being fully illuminated along a pathway to complete freedom. It is obvious that the true spiritual fiber that was engrained in the traditions of our founding fathers has been tragically lost.

Under this newfound interest in spiritualism, it is also easier for movements that were once considered primitive to bask in the light. Christian Day, a self-professing warlock and activist for Salem's Coven of the Raven Moon, was recently upset over actor Charlie Sheen's negative comments about witches. He wanted to clear the confusion by announcing to America that his coven would be releasing 'positive spirits' in Charlie's direction. Warlocks are 'enlightened' individuals according to Day. Religious tolerance was never dangerous to an American society grounded in Christian theology. However, the further America travels from its Christian roots, the deeper it delves into mystical practices. This is treacherous.

The greatest danger is that the political climate has watered down man's perspective of God. As a culture, we no longer fear God, which removes the basic foundation of wisdom (Psalm 111:10). The great influx of multiple nationalities ushers in numerous beliefs so quickly that the church cannot keep up. A population that holds little respect toward God is swiftly building. The church cannot ignore this trend. The world grows rapidly around us, and the spirit of the age pushes and peddles its evil agenda among the masses. The church must not remain silent. People are hungry for truth, and if we sit silently, they will find all the wrong answers. Despite the echoing sentiments, there is still but one answer, one door, one way, and that is the way of the cross. The truth is still found only in Jesus Christ.

We have lived lackadaisically because it is all that we know. We use the five senses as ultimate reality. Like Thomas, we long to touch in order to determine what is real. We want to know the end from the beginning of every endeavor. We want to walk for God without faith. We would rather stand on intuition and embrace the instability of feeling. Men allowing emotions to rule is one of the world's greatest threats. It is also one of God's greatest disappointments concerning His church. The overall stagnancy and lack of understanding of His people is alarming.

We mistakenly devalue important matters by placing emphasis on issues of lessor importance. We encourage and embrace our religion and doctrine. These are important, but neither should be defended to the point of losing a relationship with God. Numerical and financial gain has increasingly replaced the importance of apostolic power, anointing, and authority. Plans and programs have replaced the necessity of risk taking that has always been the sheer essence of living by faith. Inner holiness has been the focus of many, while outward holiness has declined. Vice versa, others have been so protective and proactive concerning outward holiness that inner sanctification has become an imperative of the past. True holiness has been forgotten, as we have lost intimacy with God. The love of Christ has been weakened; for selfless love can never be fully present where human nature rules. The true manifestation of Godly love comes only when man commits to dying daily.

Man's kingdom must give way to the greater purpose of

God's Kingdom. The tragedy is that we view a portrait that is greater and more everlasting, while at the same time failing to grasp the magnitude of the Kingdom. We realize the existence of a permanent and principal lifestyle, but we fail to view it on God's terms. When man views God's purpose through human perception, it only minimizes and devalues God's sovereignty.

We mistakenly view the Kingdom through the lens and spectrum of our government. Political knowledge is far different from the understanding by which God created His universe. Man's concepts do nothing but rob God of His authority, power, majesty, and rule over humanity. This is perfectly acceptable for many Christians, because we don't like to submit human will except to personal agendas. Surrendering to another principle diminishes humanity, which goes against man's nature. We must learn to see God on His own terms.

In his number one best seller, *God's Politics*, Jim Wallis reminded us that God is not American. God doesn't play by our rules. He's not dictated to or defined by our concepts of government. He's not concerned with political agendas. He doesn't have a panel He turns to for advice and intelligence. When God decides to move, He moves. When He decides to stop, He stops. When He opens the door, it is forever open. When He closes it, it remains closed. God is in complete control of every facet of the known world and all that remains undiscovered beyond. Even though belittled and downgraded by human minds, there has been no actual disintegration of God. He is as colossal, powerful, and matchless as He has ever been.

Modern legalistic views are misguided. One of man's gravest mistakes is to try and make God like us instead of becoming more like Him. However, our tendency is to view Him through the broken lenses of flawed humanity. We often humanize God instead of deify Him.

We want a modern god. We demand a god that only demonstrates mercy, not one that requires respect and integrity. We want a god to repair reproach and heal hurts, not one that demands action and service. We desire an ancient god of war to protect against evil and execute judgment on those who trespass against us. However, we desire a contemporary god that values the current world system when it comes to our own lives. We want to "serve" God on human terms, which means that we want Him to serve us. This will never happen with Jesus.

GOD IS SOVEREIGN

God is sovereign. The world, the universe, every prospective horizon; God is the Supreme Ruler over it all. We inexplicably know this to be true. However, we only consider and respect one side of His sovereignty now. We focus on God's overcoming prowess. We love the fact that God reigns over every enemy of my life.

However, we no longer contemplate His right to rule our lives. It doesn't rest well with modern humanistic views concerning control of one's own destiny and reigning over free will. The information era has robbed the church of faith, carefully replacing faith with knowledge. Most men no longer respond to God's call without over-evaluating the price. Undertaking tasks solely because God declared it is rare today. We assume God has not adjusted to our more fast paced and aggressive lifestyles, somehow thinking God no longer has the ability to finish whatever endeavor He starts. We want to know the risk versus the reward of everything God asks. The calculators constantly click, as we are consumed with the concept of cost.

However, if one continually considers cost, it is an indication that he has never fully surrendered. Once self has been fully laid on the altar, there is no more sacrifice to measure. Nothing God asks is too much.

In discussions with the late apostle Billy Cole, the tremendous sacrifice that both he and his precious wife, Sis. Shirley Cole, made through the years was highly apparent. His contribution to the Kingdom of God is arguably unparalleled in modern times, and many would argue even surpasses the lives of the apostle Paul and evangelistic Peter.

However, despite his credentials, many men discredit his work because of the incredible numbers reported overseas concerning miracles and people receiving the Holy Ghost. However, he and others at these massive crusades account that they greatly downplayed the numbers reported because they had no desire to over-represent what was taking place. They chose to err on the side of caution.

Others dishonor the magnitude of his life by stating that he was unbalanced. They claim that he was "too committed" to the Kingdom. Bro. Cole spoke openly about mistakes he had made and choices he wished he could revisit, but he never spoke regretfully about what had been accomplished for the Kingdom of God. He encouraged us to not be so involved with the Kingdom that we forget to bring the Kingdom to our own families. He spoke about the importance of compassion and love.

Shortly before his passing, Apostle Cole spoke in-depth about love. He reminded the apostolic movement about the necessity of returning to evangelism and revival. He told how he had performed many mighty works under God's anointing, yet he had failed to learn how to truly love. He pleaded with the church to combine his passion for the Kingdom with a passion for the lost. His last message was probably his most powerful. Other messages changed lives and saved souls for the Kingdom, but his final message would transform the Kingdom itself, if believers recognize the force in his words and commit to living it.

Sister Cole, with tears in her eyes as distant memories traced through her mind, spoke of the sacrifices they had both made. She discussed how she'd given so much that it literally affected her health. Is it any wonder that these two precious people have impacted more lives for God than any couple that has ever lived? They both understood and were committed to the Kingdom. They had both placed their lives on the altar without ever looking back. God is searching for men and women with this pedigree. Men who will learn from this great apostle's admitted mistakes but live with his same passion and willingness to sacrifice.

However, it is difficult to find such commitment today. The information era has added to the dysfunction in that we demand every detail from doctrine. Why am I required to comply to certain rules. Immediately, we consider holiness when discussing this issue, but holiness is not the only avenue to which this applies. Many times, God speaks on behalf of the Kingdom and calls a believer to engage in His will, but the believer waits for others to accomplish the task. Often, believers are either too preoccupied or too afraid at the cost. Too often, people demand answers, and the believer will not move until all answers are adequately met. After careful contemplation and thorough inspection, if God's plan will not require too much stress, sacrifice, financial hardship, or inconvenience, God's will is enacted. Of course, this comes after a board meeting is called or family discussion held, for the more natural support mustered, the easier it is to skid into following God's plan.

The quandary is that we've tried to strip God of His sovereignty, which will never be allowed. God is still highest. To be apostolic, we must learn to unapologetically live for Christ. Scripture reveals this concept when the centurion came to Jesus in need of a miracle. Jesus offered to go to the man's home to meet the need. The man, understanding authority, told Jesus that it wouldn't be necessary to make the journey. If Jesus would just speak the word, the centurion was convinced the miracle would be accomplished. This man understood that Jesus is in charge. He understood the concept of absolute Sovereignty. If the Sovereign (Ruler) spoke it, it would be accomplished, because the Sovereign has dominion.

In America, we are used to officials being elected into office. We understand that if we elected them, we can also, after the appropriate time, un-elect them. We have pastors living by the same rules. We voted them into office. Therefore, if we can stir up enough trouble, we can vote them out. Every time men are placed over others, there's a system of checks and balances that protect those under authority by restricting the power of those in ruling positions. God does not play fairly by these self-imposed rules that we attempt to force on Him.

God has never been concerned with approval ratings. It rains on the just and unjust alike. He isn't campaigning for allegiance. Good things happen to sinful people. Unpleasant things happen to decent people. Life happens to us all. God's not affected by man's opinion. He isn't swayed by cultural trends or societal views. He has a purpose. He has the means to make it happen. He has the authority to ensure it does.

The principal conflict is that because God is sovereign, He doesn't have to explain every detail to His followers. That's the essence of faith. One cannot know all the details and possess faith at the same time. Faith is evidence of things not seen. God doesn't need to seek my advice on how to manage my life. He's in charge of it. He doesn't owe me anything just because I live for Him. My life is not my own. He's not obligated because I go to church and worship Him. He is God alone. He is the immortal, and I am the mortal. That will never change.

Humans are so self-pleasing and fickle. We rejoice about God being the King of Kings and Lord of Lords when it's convenient. When He brings His omniscience and might into my troubling situation, I take no issue with it. If His ability carries me through the trials of life, I desire His presence. However, I do not wish to give Him the same credence when

He demands my action on behalf of His Kingdom. I don't want to give Him full authority as Alpha and Omega, when He's requiring that I do something that others will think is ridiculous. He's not King of Kings when He requires real sacrifice. However, it doesn't matter how what He asks of me affects family, disrupts social networks, dents bank accounts, disrupts financial security, or messes with well thought out plans; He is just as sovereign then as He has ever been. His sincere request should cause a believer to erupt into action. There is no consequence too fanatical if one has committed their life to God and then recognizes His voice.

American life has fattened the church. Many are too naturally blessed to make a difference. Earthly blessings often propel one toward a state of apathy and tolerance that are detrimental to effectively benefiting those around us on a spiritual level. The natural blessings make us forget God's plans that are conceptually bigger than all of us.

HIS KINGDOM

It amounts to an uncomfortable matter of faith. Humanity does not embrace true sovereignty because it forces us to submit and sacrifice. Often, we fail to sell out to God because we do not have the faith to let go of personal positions, ideas, finances, dreams, goals, and abilities in order to do whatever God requests. We do not truly advance the Kingdom because we are self-prohibited by the concept of a King.

I'm not devaluing the concept of the King by any means.

We must understand that God is not some symbolic figurehead over an empty empire. He is eternally significant, and His purpose is perpetually perfect. God cannot be separated from His Kingdom. Therefore, to fight for the King means that I must fight for His Kingdom. To love the King means that I must love the Kingdom. To live for the King means that I must also live for the Kingdom. There's no way to separate them.

Over 150 times, the New Testament mentions the Kingdom in regards to God's system of government on this earth. Matthew demonstrated that God could not be separated from the Kingdom, as he talked about Christ's Gospel, and then called it the Gospel of the Kingdom (Matthew 4:23). Peter and Paul preached about Jesus in the book of Acts, as they spread the gospel of the Kingdom. It is apparent, according to the Bible, that the message of Christ and the message of the Kingdom are one and the same.

Christ, as a twelve-year-old, provides further evidence that the King and the Kingdom cannot be separated. At such a young age, Jesus was already making the distinction that He had to do the 'business' of His father. Jesus presented the concept that some things are more serious than everyday life.

In His powerful sermon, the Beatitudes, Jesus said that God and the Kingdom are one. Four times He instructed His audience that living the life He was prescribing would establish the Kingdom of God in their midst. We know this is speaking of literally bringing God's presence into theirs.

Twice during His teaching of the Lord's Prayer, Jesus

mentioned the importance of the Kingdom. He instructed them to pray that the Kingdom would come to earth, ushering in the power of Heaven. He also closed the prayer by reminding everyone of God's absolute supremacy. "For thine is the Kingdom, and the power, and the glory forever. Amen," (Matthew 6:13).

According to Scripture, believers should love God above all else. The second commandment is to love other people the way we love ourselves. On these two laws hinge all other laws and every word of the prophets (Mark 12:30-31).

Was Jesus then being sacrilegious when He suggested that man seek the Kingdom of God first, even above the first law to seek God? Absolutely not. Jesus was again demonstrating that these two concepts are the same. We are to love God with all our heart, soul, mind, and strength. If we love God to that dimension, we will put His Kingdom first.

The King and the Kingdom cannot be separated. If one devalues the King, he also devalues the Kingdom. However, the opposite is also true, if one devalues the Kingdom, he also devalues the King. A passionate pursuit of Christ should always lead to a Kingdom focus.

Jesus attempted to get mankind to understand this principle. Parable after parable He compared the Kingdom of Heaven to different concepts that people could understand. He tried to get men from every walk of life to embrace not only Him but also His purpose. He tried to create a desire within men to love Him, but to also love His will. It's easy to love a distant and devoted King; it is much harder to engage His Kingdom.

Jesus didn't just preach it. He also demonstrated it through His life. It was most exemplified in the manner of His death. On the way to the cross, beaten and mercilessly abused, Jesus had to confront thoughts that could've caused Him to remove Himself from the agony He was enduring.

He was a warrior King who came in the form of a humble servant. He could easily call down angels to destroy His tormentors. However, as His accusers questioned him, His reply to their mocking accusations sent ripples through the cosmos, forever changing the landscape of human interaction with eternal purpose. He uttered the words,

"My kingdom is not of this world."

He acknowledged, "I can endure because I have a focus that is not 'me' centered. My focus is on the Kingdom."

Even in intense pain, Jesus would not separate Himself from Heaven's everlasting empire. If the church is going to be apostolic in nature and return to authority and power in these final hours, it must engage the Kingdom with the fervor of Christ. We must live for both the King and His Kingdom.

KINGDOM APPLICATION

The question every Christian should ask is "Where does the Kingdom fit into my life?" If we say we live for the King, but aren't connected to and active in His Kingdom, we're living a lie. To live for God on human terms and minimize His purpose is to not live for Him at all.

The Kingdom must be applied on more than just an inspirational level. God's purpose cannot be removed because it is spiritual, and humanity is sinful by nature. Any belief or entity that separates the King from His Kingdom only devalues the King and makes His purpose obsolete.

> **Our power is in the King, but our purpose is in the Kingdom.**

A King with nothing to rule over is not truly in power. He cannot reign if He has nothing to oversee. The very fact that God is indeed sovereign leads to the conclusion that the Kingdom is of utmost importance.

The danger is that it's easy to waver one way or the other when trying to live for God effectively under modern evangelistic rules. It is far too effortless to envelop ourselves under the auspice of the King while devaluing the Kingdom. Any belief that is all power (King) and no purpose (Kingdom) is too strong and will only destroy. However, the opposite also holds true. It's easy to engage the Kingdom and the work of the church without ever entering into a relationship with the King. Any belief that's all purpose (Kingdom) and no power (King) is too weak and cannot stand. We need both the power and purpose.

We can no longer afford to be lackadaisical in our efforts to reach the lost. Living with a Kingdom purpose demands that we become actively engaged in reaching people. God is concerned about every person living outside of a relationship with Him. The very reason He died was to destroy the works of the devil and to save others. The purpose of the Kingdom is the same. The church must become more proficient at finding, saving, and retaining those who are lost in the vicious cycle of sin. It's certainly imperative that we become active in reaching the world by apostolic standards.

Christ's commission to His church underlines the importance of this mission. He promised that power from on high would overtake believers as they were filled with the Holy Ghost. However, He did not stop there. After the (power), He commissioned them to go into the entire world and preach the gospel (purpose). The early church was birthed directly from a union between passion, power, and purpose. Without a proper balance of these three, the promise of apostolic power will never occur. The prophetic utterances of long ago will only come to pass when believers engage the Kingdom and the King to the point that promise, passion, power, and purpose collide.

The purpose of the Kingdom was about you before you were saved. However, once a person is saved, a transition transpires. The Kingdom stops being about us, and we must start being about the Kingdom. Once, the Kingdom existed to serve us, to capture us from a life of bondage. However, salvation freed us from that bondage. Now, we are to walk in a newness of life, a newness that causes us to live for the Kingdom. Like a twelve-year-old Jesus, we must be about the Father's business.

POOR REPRESENTATION

The problem many Christians encounter is the discovery that we're an extremely poor image of God. Like a house of trick mirrors, the image we give is at best distorted and tainted. However, God has never asked us to be the image; He has simply propositioned us to reflect the image. We are not to pretend to live perfect lives. We are to live such transparent lives that when others look, they see Jesus.

True transparency means that one hides nothing. It means a life free from immoral failure, because there's no room for such indiscretions. It means a life free from accusation, for everyone knows that there's been no place for negligent sin to occur.

Integrity and honesty collide with selfish desires and impure motives at the point of representing Christ. One can have the form of Godliness, but if the thoughts and intents of the heart are impure, the external gives a remarkably poor likeness of God. It is only when one changes the heart to the point of true conversion that we truly reflect Christ to others. Good deeds, selfless acts, and kind words are necessary. However, none are pure indicators of a person's portrayal of God. Only a heart change at the level of intimacy between God and man can produce the depiction God desires.

God hates when Christian's misrepresent Him. He desires for His church to depict Him in the fullness of His authority and power. Only an apostolic person can personify Christ this way. Enticing words, well laid programs, beautiful edifices, proper leadership training, and kind dispositions only go so far toward demonstrating God. Alone, these details do not display the true image of Jesus. If a church isn't changing lives, chasing demonic influence, destroying the yoke of Satan, cleansing the stain of sin, and compelling people to yield their lives, it does not typify Him. The church must cease representing its members and leaders and return to representing Christ.

God noticed that some of his people were misrepresenting themselves in the marketplace (Deuteronomy 25: 13-15). He didn't notice this misrepresentation in the temple. The people were following the rules of worship and praise. However, in the midst of fixing many of their issues, God made this decree.

> *13 Thou shalt not have in thy bag divers weights, a great and a small.*
>
> *14 Thou shalt not have in thine house divers measures, a great and a small.*
>
> *15 But thou shalt have a perfect and just weight, a perfect and just measure shalt thou have: that thy days may be lengthened in the land which the LORD thy God giveth thee.*

God created a law to deal with businessmen in the marketplace that were more interested in growing their own business than truly helping others. These men would use different weights and measuring tools to gain advantage over potential customers. If the men were purchasing items, they would use a lesser weight, so they could get product at a lower price. If selling merchandise, they would use a greater weight, to give less but demand a greater price. Both weights looked the same, so customers were unaware of the deception.

When viewing the grandiose picture of eternity, that doesn't seem significant. Other people were murdering in the streets, disrespecting the priesthood, and neglecting ministerial duties. Some gossiped. Others did illegal narcotics. Some fornicated with foreign women, performing sexually deviant acts to worship idol gods. Some men cursed His name. Why in the midst of so many problems did God address the way men measured in the marketplace?

The most fundamental perspective of this law was that kingdom business is conducted in the marketplace. The marketplace is where the reality of the kingdom takes place. It's the nuts and bolts of the kingdom, the financial and social commerce, and if one enters that area with false pretenses and personal agendas, it's dangerous to everyone involved.

God was angry about the attitude of misrepresentation. He couldn't allow it to continue. Everything He was building in the Old Testament was to be an example of what He wanted His Kingdom to become. If He allowed men to misrepresent who they were, then one day they would misrepresent who they were in Him. The result of that would be far more deadly.

God still hates it when we enter the "marketplace" and misrepresent who we are. When we live outside the church walls, where He conducts business, to establish personal kingdoms; God is not pleased. Subconsciously, many Christians come to church, reach into our bags, and pull out longer measuring tapes, because we are supposed to be more spiritual at church. However, when we get outside, we quietly pull out shorter measuring tapes. We aren't so spiritual there.

We try not to sin openly, because we fear others knowing who we really are. We don't accomplish much for the Kingdom. The problem with small weights in the marketplace is that we aren't serving our purpose. This is also a sin (James 4:17).

God wants a church that will be spiritual where man needs it most, outside the church walls. He isn't incarcerated to a building or logo. Jesus did not go to the temple for any reason other than to devote Himself to His Father. He never encountered a person in need on the street, and then talked them into attending His local assembly so their needs could be met.

Jesus took His anointing with Him when He walked out of the temple doors. People are out there with grave needs every day. We pass them and fail to recognize these needs. Could it be we are not even looking, because perhaps if we noticed, the Holy Ghost in us would demand action? By necessity faith would be challenged, and perhaps we are afraid of what we would find, if we honestly faced the challenge of being truly apostolic.

We are afraid to consider a God who always healed outside of the church. Many of us are afraid to tell others that they could healed right where they are. We don't want to talk about that, because someone may ask us to perform. We don't talk about a God who delivers from drugs, alcohol, and oppression; because we may be called on to meet someone in a moment of need, without the support of the local assembly. The sad reality is that too few of us have the relationship with God required to create a reality of apostolic authority. We don't have the power to back up the proclamation.

Therefore, we remain content to misrepresent who we are in the marketplace, the place we frequent most. God desires for His people to create balance in this unstable world.

> *A false balance is abomination to the LORD: but a just weight is his delight.*
>
> *Proverbs 11:1*
>
> *A king that sitteth in the throne of judgment scattereth away all evil with his eyes.*
>
> *Who can say, I have made my heart clean, I am pure from my sin?*
>
> *Divers weights, and divers measures, both of them are alike abomination to the LORD*
>
> *Proverbs 20:8-10*

God dealt with Solomon, "Be who you are. Present yourselves true. Do not be at odds with yourself. Quit living two different lives depending on where you are. Be who I have called you to be."

We always equate this to the arena of sin. However, God took it much deeper. He stated, "Do not come into my house and pretend that the Kingdom is the most important thing in your life, then go to the marketplace with a different weight and standard. If the Kingdom is first when you are in the church building, it should also be first in the market place.

You must prioritize me, and the way to do that is by prioritizing my Kingdom. You must use the same weights and measures in both places."

This is why Jesus emphasized that the last-day church would have a difficult time reaching people. The difficulty would lie in the church's misunderstanding of a Kingdom concept. The Kingdom is not about saved people. The Kingdom is about the lost. It's about a group of men and women that realize how blessed they are and refuse to keep that blessing to themselves. It's about men and women who decide to engage their own world, as individuals, as families, and as a church. It's about people who become concerned with making a difference where they have personal influence. The Kingdom consists of living with apostolic anointing in the "marketplaces" of our individual lives.

The real issue is not that people are disinterested in changing their lives. The concern isn't that people are no longer interested in Christianity. Recent questions addressed to the un-churched indicate that over seventy percent said they would have a discussion about the Bible and God if someone directly asked. Sixty percent said they would accept a Bible study if someone seemed interested in teaching them. Overwhelming results indicate that people would allow a Christian to pray for them if approached during a time of crisis.

I spent two days asking people in a community with a large Pentecostal church if they had ever been invited to a service. This church has been established in its community for several years. Tragically, only twenty-eight percent responded that they had ever been invited to this apostolic church. It continued to grow internally, but the membership hadn't learned the value of taking God outside of the walls. It's an indicator that people talk to who they know, but rarely extend beyond their own comfort zones to engage the lost in the marketplace of life.

Sadly, the issue is not that sinners are no longer interested in the Kingdom. The issue is that the church is no longer interested in the Kingdom. At times, we're intoxicated with the King and what He can do for us, but if we do not engage in His business, we are missing the purpose that we're supposed to undertake. Churches remain un-apostolic in nature merely because its members continue to look and think inwardly. Anytime people are into maintenance more than growth there can be NO apostolic move of God. Church services remain in the muck of mediocrity because services are designed to minister within. As long as members come to church with a mentality of "getting" instead of "giving," apostolic moves of the Spirit will continue to be obstructed. As long as the only powerful demonstrations of God's Spirit occur hidden behind manmade walls, the church will fail to be apostolic in nature.

PARABLE OF WAGES

There is a story in Scripture that has always been confounding. It's the parable of the householder that went out early to hire men to work in his vineyard. He hired the first group for a penny a day (hopefully that was a lot back then). Three hours later the householder returned to the market place and found more men standing idle. He hired those men to work in the vineyard. This same process occurred every three hours, until finally eleven hours after his first hire, he returned to the marketplace and found more idle men. He then asked the question,

"Why are you just standing here idle all day?"

They replied that they hadn't been hired, so he hired them. At the end of the day, all of the men came to receive their wages, and all of the men were surprised when they were all paid the same. Those who worked all day received the same amount as those who had only worked a few hours. Naturally, the men who had worked all day were extremely disgruntled. However, the owner of the vineyard rebuked them.

This story has never seemed fair. It has always been a parable of unjust wages. I never understood the principle that Jesus was trying to get across. However, that's because I've always looked at this parable through the eyes of a man thinking from his own selfish mentality. It's only when looking through the eyes of the Kingdom that this parable makes sense.

This parable is not a parable of unjust wages at all; it's a parable of the harvest. Jesus wanted people to understand,

"You stand idle in the marketplace. What must I do to engage you in the harvest?"

I believe Jesus was saying, "My main concern is not the ill feelings of idle workers. My main concern is not the emotions of active laborers. My main concern is the harvest. Will you prioritize the harvest? I will so whatever is necessary to reach the lost."

The most noteworthy aspect of proving one's love for God is to develop an attitude equal to the urgency of the hour. He doesn't want us to just fall in love with Him, but if we love Him, we must fall in love with the harvest. If we are to serve Him, we must serve the harvest.

As apostolic reapers, if we're concerned about the harvest like He is, we wouldn't be upset about wages (benefits). We wouldn't be concerned about the amount of sacrifice required to complete the task. Idle laborers, if we were as concerned about the harvest as He is, He wouldn't have to search to get us into the fields. We would already be outside the church walls and in the community.

In order to be apostolic in nature and to witness apostolic results, we must first become apostolic in a passion for Kingdom purpose. God is calling us to recommit to Him through a recommitment to Kingdom principles. The measure of how in love with God I am is not how much I pray or worship. It is discovered in how much I actively invest in His Kingdom. It is determined by how much I'm willing to sacrifice in pursuit of Him and the lost. Am I impacting my world with His?

The church must stop being so judgmental if it is to truly affect the harvest. It's far easier to build a bridge from beams than from splinters. Every believer must recognize his or her own faults and judge his or her own sins only. Show mercy to the undeserving. Embrace the unlovable with true compassion. Forgive when it seems impossible. Only then will people desire to connect, for they will recognize something supernatural. For once they will not just see your faith or religion. They will see JESUS!

7
ABSOLUTES OF CONVENIENCE

Differences in generational philosophies must be examined if the gap between two ever-widening methods is to be bridged. Unfortunately, as is often the case, the role of the vocal minority significantly influences the understanding of the less vocal majority. This has become an apparent problem as the modern church struggles to free itself from hindrances that have caused stagnation, keeping it from becoming the powerful entity that God intended.

An excited, youthful generation marches forward, desperately desiring to experience the revival of yesteryear, while foolishly demanding it on their terms. An elder generation observes in pessimistic anticipation the dreadful scene of declining morality they fear is inevitable. The dilemma is that each side is right in what it believes. Fear exists in the elders because a few misguided people have masqueraded as prophetic voices while puppeteering for personal agendas. On the other side, a few disgruntled voices lead the charge of "apostolic" living that's too harsh and judgmental and only antagonizes the modern view of love for lost humanity.

Despite the beliefs of many, there is still a younger generation that's not looking to discard doctrine. In most cases, there are no misguided motives manipulatively trying to replace truth. Most young people with a heart to serve God are not devaluing long established principles. They are engaging culture in a more modern style, but most are not denying time-honored apostolic foundations.

The confusion comes because of a generational disconnect. We have entered the demanding era of information. Any subject can be easily and freely researched. Technological advancements have made learning much more engaging and informative. The demands placed on children in most educational systems are more rigorous. The average "C" student still possesses more knowledge than did the "A" student from a decade ago.

These factors have created a culture that demands knowledge. Details that seem trivial under prior generational mentalities are extremely pertinent to today's young believers. If they are going to engage their world, they must be equipped with answers.

That is why most young people ask "why." It's not out of disrespect or unbelief, but a genuine curiosity. Most are not satisfied to merely believe. Every standard taught is not scripturally provable, as some have their origins in contemporary wisdom. Most young ministers understand that leeway had to be given, not for personal interpretation, but for sound judgment. However, despite this understanding, most still wish to understand the conventional wisdom. Most young ministers have a healthy respect for those who have established the freedom we now enjoy, and in many cases, questions arise merely from a desire to learn from the past.

Sadly, this isn't always the case. There has been an alarming movement within younger generations attempting to discredit many sacred beliefs. This minority must not be the only young voices recognized. There are still many who believe the doctrines of Scripture just as strongly as the elders who created them. The traditions and heritage of the church aren't in as much peril as many suppose. Many young ministers would fight and die defending established apostolic doctrine.

However, just as this rebellious faction appears to be the voice of most young ministers, previous generations had a few that promoted personal agendas from public platforms as well. This dogma was shoved foolishly at many people who did not fully understand the doctrine. In that era, "why" was not nearly as weighty as "what." People unquestioningly followed instructions given. This created a breakdown in the area of Biblical knowledge. Many people lived holiness and Biblical doctrine to near perfection, yet never understood why. Honor must be paid to these people who lived as their culture dictated. They lived a life of consecration that's often unparalleled today, and God honored their commitment and sacrifice.

However, the vocal minority from previous generations pushed agendas that made doctrine out of details. This led to a disintegration of compassion that birthed congregations of condemnation. People of varying philosophies even held spirited debates, creating a competitive nature that led to the establishment of "absolutes" that were convenient to further personal agendas. The result was too many shades of gray in pictures supposed to be black and white.

This lack of knowledge was fine, until it collided with the impassable barrier of a generation demanding answers. The younger (knowledge based) generations started questioning and many in the elder (commitment based) generations responded with rebukes as to why the sudden interrogations. This led to a group of impatient young ministers trying to find answers to better equip themselves to engage their culture. However, they unknowingly began to devalue previous generational theology. Since the vocal minority from prior generations were more stringent on issues of holiness and doctrine, the vocal minority of the younger generations set out to prove how many of these issues do not truly relate to salvation. The more "absolutes" discovered "false," the more this vocal minority seeks to eliminate all absolutes. This presiding attitude has created within the elder generations a stigma toward youthful ones, who for the most part, truly desire more of God and want to be led into apostolic ministry by those who have already been there.

TRUE ABSOLUTES

The danger facing the younger generation is the tendency to throw the baby out with the bath water. There are many absolutes in living for God, but there are no absolutes of convenience. God has always demanded sacrifice, excellence, commitment, and spiritual progress over carnal appeasement. These principles weigh heavy on man's nature. They cannot be lived accidentally or halfheartedly. They must exist with holy purpose and passion. We cannot generate absolutes of convenience to support ideas that do nothing but birth false hardship that creates judgmental spirits.

Holiness living is still an absolute. A righteous lifestyle in dress, mannerisms, actions, and attitude is still mandated by God. Women's clothing designed to stimulate man's sexual nature still repulses God. That has not and will never change. Society does not set the standards for what is acceptable and not acceptable in God's Kingdom. Living a step above the world is not the defining line of holiness. It never has been. Only a holy God has the right to designate standards of holiness for His people. God's Word alone defines immodesty.

A few vocal young ministers have stated that if we are to reach the lost more effectively, we must rid ourselves of doctrinal hardships. However, love without sacrifice is not Biblical. True tolerance is not blindly declaring that all absolutes are negotiable. It is not about blindly making sin and ungodliness acceptable.

True tolerance is about standing for what's right within the body of Christ, while lovingly accepting those outside of the body. It's about being patient as we reach others with the message of Jesus. Tolerance should not be feared because it is misapplied. In reality, it's a tool that Jesus used when dealing with those who were counter culture to the Kingdom.

When one plays by different rules than the natural world, opposition is inevitable. True tolerance teaches that love extends no matter a person's current or past standing. It's not an acceptance of man's sinful nature. It's an acceptance of the person, while seeing them not as they are, but as they can be through Christ.

Tolerance and compassion are closely related. Once moved with compassion toward the predicament of a person without God, tolerance must be activated. It's an extension of grace, giving others the benefit of the doubt, even when their actions have determined that they do not deserve it. Jesus demonstrated this many times, as He would touch a person and meet their needs; then gently encourage them to continue void of the sinful actions that had caused their hardship. There were no guarantees that they'd continue in perfection after He left, but he simply extended grace and operated in tolerance. We must become like Jesus.

DOCTRINAL DISPUTES

Age-old arguments always find their way into every generation. Having previously failed, the enemy counters by attacking leaders who were too young to remember prior battles. That's why young leaders must be well connected to elders who remember the struggles of yesteryear.

Every spiritual age must face the questions. The lines indicating intricate boundaries must be clearly established. Every generation must realize that walking in the shadows of yesterday's heroes is not enough. The transition must occur. The mantle must be dropped. The front lines of the battlefield must be inundated with fresh faces. However, in positioning with prior eras, new leaders must find the delicate balance of neither blindly following the way of others nor seeking to devalue old truths while seeking fresh direction. They must learn the voice of God.

God often instructs one to continue down the road already traveled. There is no room for young leaders claiming submission to God while continually dabbling in "new" doctrine. Repentance is still a Biblical, theologically sound doctrine. It is still an essential part of the Plan of Salvation. True repentance is a complete turning away from a sinful nature and turning toward God.

Modern theology attempts to reduce repentance to an apologetic outcry of those caught in sin. However, saying "I'm sorry" after the same continued failure is not what God intended. Apostolic men and women understand that true repentance brings a life change that eliminates the opportunity for recurring failure. Without true repentance, the Kingdom of Heaven will never be realized.

Water baptism, by immersion in the Name of Jesus, is still a vital part of the Plan of Salvation. It's not just an action associating believers through symbolic connection. It's not some secret rite of passage euphorically bonding believers. It's the cleansing of the old sinful stains of carnal living, and the opportunity for a sinner to start over.

The infilling of the Holy Ghost is still the only way of Salvation. These principles are nonnegotiable. Every generation challenges the validity of these claims. However, age-to-age, the truth has prevailed.

The writer of Corinthians warned that it was necessary for false doctrine to arise (I Corinthians 11:19). Paul later warned Timothy that seducing spirits would lead many astray with false doctrine in the last days (I Timothy 4:1). However, the tone of these messages was not one of gloom. The writer told the church at Corinth that the heresy would produce a manifestation of the true sons of God. The steadfastness of some in the new generation to stand for truth is what will separate them from the pack. The sons of God do not make themselves known by the prayers they pray or miracles they produce. They make themselves known by willingly upholding the doctrine.

THE ABSOLUTE OF INTERNAL HOLINESS

The true meaning of holiness is often lost in external views that separate Christian viewpoints and cause obvious lines of distinction. Many "holiness" people are holy in detail and outward array, but inwardly lack the nature of God.

Most people who have been in Christianity for a few years have little problem with "holiness." Holiness has become academic, in principle, if not in practice. However, as the knowledge of holiness has increased, the practical application of it has dramatically shifted. At the center is a focus on creed rather than companionship. Without God, there is no holiness, regardless of laws observed.

Convenience, in this case, is not as it would appear. To outsiders, it seems inconvenient to live the holiness virtues of most Christian theology. However, to devout believers, this inconvenience is worth the sacrifice. True inconvenience comes in submitting attitudes to God. However, this too is holiness.

> **It is time to quit playing the part and start being the part.**

The danger of falling to the absolutes of convenience is ever present. The little foxes destroy the vineyard, causing many to be lost while looking the part they feel prepares them for the rapture. They are drones who never understand why they live the way they do. While mocking other denominations that are "steeped in ritualism," they ignore their own traditional behavior. They play their roles well, wearing uniforms of sanctity. However, behind the pious masquerade, they idly sit, void of power, anointing, and passion. Despite their best efforts at religious perfection, they have little impact in their world.

Perhaps it is time to quit playing the part and start being the part. If the power to heal and overcome darkness is not evident in the believer, there's an obvious disconnect. The signs of true spirituality are not dress codes and bylaws. These are necessary and Biblically sound. However, the true signs of spirituality are much subtler: sacrifice, loving others, discipline, inner peace, willingness to extend mercy and grace, and patience. These virtues become vices because they cannot be adequately measured. Human nature is to seek personal approval that builds emotional security. It's easier to seek man's approval than God's, for God's approval isn't as clearly defined. Therefore, men design "absolutes" of convenience that define "holiness" on their terms, while ignoring it on God's terms. Playing by Christian rules, it's easy to appease judgmental people. However, man forgets God's agenda in the chaos. Regardless of how inconvenient it seems, man must return to the origin of holiness, which is an intimate relationship with God first.

8
THE CHURCH'S RESPONSE TO THE FAMILY PARADIGM SHIFT

The enemy's vicious onslaught against the family is no secret. Any Christian claiming spirituality while denying the effects of a strategic onslaught against the family isn't paying attention. Commitment to marriage is marginal. Kids are raising themselves, in the world and the church. Adults justify their negligent parenting habits by making excuses for their children instead of disciplining them. Under the auspice of trust, children are allowed to make monumental decisions that profoundly impact their life. Some families may be heavily involved in religious activities but live in worldly pleasure outside of the church. This is confusing to children still in the foundational stages of Christian existence.

Sin is more prevalent in the church today than ever before. It's just better hidden. True holiness has been replaced by an inner bedlam masquerading as godliness by way of external discipline. Fathers, who have the responsibility of spiritually protecting their families, are severely limited in spiritual discernment. Far too often women have become the dominant spiritual leaders in Christian homes, creating an imbalance that God never intended. The church has addressed these issues by severely overcompensating. The results of such shifting dynamics run counter to God's original plan and aid in the family structure's drastic decline.

A dilemma arises when one must determine where life stops being about God and starts becoming about church, for any belief that belittles eternal purpose for temporary principle is not of God. God desires families that actively engage His Kingdom.

Family dynamics are of utmost importance. There's a Godly call for families to engage in the pursuit of God and to work for the benefit of the Kingdom together. There was never supposed to be a competition between family dynamics and Kingdom living. Rather, the early church unleashed a call reminding fathers that Jesus Christ and His Kingdom are the absolute most essential ingredients to ensure family preservation. Engaging the family in the importance of the Kingdom brings a unity and closeness that cannot be grafted by playing games and spending time together. The protection of Scripture comes to families who do the work of the Father.

Quality time is significant, and every family should have

fun making lifelong memories. Everything should not be laced in spirituality and carefully interwoven with divine principles. There should be many memories that extend beyond church walls and Kingdom concepts. However, if the vast majority of fond memories are naturally focused, they create an unbalanced view that damages the family's concept of God and His higher purpose. Creating a culture wherein children feel safe choosing anything over God's higher agenda is dangerous. Parenting is about forming patterns and establishing decision-making that makes it easier to pursue Godly fulfillment over natural appeasement.

Making "family" only about the family shortchanges those involved and short circuits God's attempts to bring greater revelation. This greater revelation comes to the family as a whole, but it interjects into each member personally. Families grow together through interaction, but they form deeper bonds through establishing common purpose. That's why crisis situations are often catalysts for the greatest growth of intimacy in families. Purpose is the great equalizer, for it always unites. The greater the purpose, the greater the unity achieved, and there is no greater purpose than God's Kingdom.

Christian parents negate some of life's greatest teaching moments because they fail to extend outward. Instruction is the first step in the introduction of knowledge. However, most people don't learn when a directive is initially given. Learning is best achieved by living it. Example is the best motivator, and experience the best teacher. The only way to ensure that children live dedicated to God (and His purpose) is to demonstrate it to them while presenting opportunities for them to experience it.

Families who have a tendency to focus only inwardly set themselves up for failure. They walk right into Satan's snare. Lucifer's narcissistic views are not only pertinent at the individual level. If he can create within families a restrictive subculture, he has effectively put a damper on the most functional unit of the church. By forcing the family focus inward, he affects both the present and the future, ensuring that coming generations naturally develop the same egocentric mindset.

It's imperative that families engage in God's higher agenda. They must go beyond the walls of both the church and the home. If revival and power begins at the familial level, then the family must climb out of its comfort zone and connect to God's plans in order to see the full effects of His supremacy. The responsibility of parents is to unify the family to God and commit to His Kingdom above all else.

RESPONSIBILITY TO THE NEXT GENERATION

Many parents cheat children out of lessons and experiences that could forever change them. Most children, even in Christian homes, aren't getting proper instruction and training concerning Godly living. Most parents feel they don't have time to properly instruct children and are even less likely to demonstrate the basics of prayer, Bible reading, and worship in the home. Many fully expect the church to educate their kids. However, today's Sunday School curriculum is less about critical factors that should be instilled from the earliest moments of life. There are fewer lessons on prayer and its power to transform lives. In fear of indoctrinating children, many have replaced lessons on practical holiness and true worship with Bible stories that have little instructional value. However, children need to be indoctrinated with truth. If the church does not do it, the world will program them with its filth from the Internet, television, movies, and radio. They are more educated about sex, homosexuality, dating, racism, and rebellious living from their peers and the media than from the only two institutions of safety they truly have, the home and the church.

Most Sunday school lessons and parental training are highly exclusive. Sunday school awards include personal offering, Scripture memorization, faithful attendance, and bringing a Bible. Most classrooms no longer offer rewards to students for bringing a friend. It's no wonder the cycle of generations continues to subtly regress in the areas of sacrifice and personal evangelism. In many cases, by the time a child reaches youth age, they've already been trained that the church is mainly concerned with its members. They've already learned that family is mostly concerned with protecting and strengthening its members as well. We would never openly admit these feelings, because outwardly expressing it sounds wrong, but it is the way we live. Many "Holiness minded" families have learned to be exclusive.

It's the responsibility of every parent to make sure their children are properly instructed about Kingdom living. The onus of liability is not and never has been on the church. The church supports efforts that should be taking place within the home. A child will seldom rise above the nonexistent lessons and horrific examples of their parents. Fathers and mothers that gossip or speak negatively about the church cannot realistically expect their children to trust the church to guide them through life. Unfortunately, this relationship between the home and the church is completely bilateral. Most children truly living for God have seen it modeled from within. However, most children who do not live for God have never seen it personally modeled. What an indictment against the modern home.

FAMILY MATTERS

Scripture strongly suggests that God takes matters of the family seriously. The New Testament warns to be sober on these issues. God has created principles that preserve the family, because it's extremely vital to Him.

Outside of Scriptural simplicity and theological platitude, even the natural world emphasizes the importance of the family. In backward attempts to sabotage the family, even Hollywood has proven this. When wanting to add drama to a main character's back-story, the character usually comes from a broken home or abusive family dynamics. Most romantic movie drama involves someone who leaves the traditional significance of family values.

Doctors, scientists, social workers, and family experts who don't even believe in God still support the notion of strengthening the family structure. They also blame the continually declining morality of America on the persistent loss of interest in strong family dynamics. Their research indicates that most socially deviant and villainous criminals come from a family that failed in transferring culturally significant mores. This lack of parental management enabled some children to commit ghastly acts of brutality. Many of the world's most malicious men, such as Adolf Hitler, serial murderers, and convicted felons, come from families that have been labeled as incredibly dysfunctional. These are strong indicators that the family unit must be strengthened.

EVOLUTIONARY PARENTING

One skill that separates humanity from the other species is the ability to teach offspring on deep levels. Human parents educate and model far more than the basic life skills of survival. This is not only expected. God demands it.

According to Scripture, man cannot judge success by accomplishments, profitable portfolios, or natural victories. The truest test of success is to look at the achievements of one's children and grandchildren. Has the mantle been passed? Have teachings been ingrained that transcend one's physical presence in their lives?

One stands to lose his or her most precious gifts if parenting outside of the incredible weight of eternity. While living in the moment, parents must utilize every chance to teach lessons of infinite consequence. Parents lose children by trying to keep them satisfied in the present, mistakenly believing that friendship will triumph. Friendship may guarantee lifelong devotion, which is a trend of selfish parenting. However, it will never substitute in matters pertaining to the Kingdom. A child's first loyalty should be toward God, not parent. However, this can only be taught if the child sees that the parent's first loyalty is God, not child.

This may sound harsh in current society's softened view on family dynamics, but to teach trust without demanding obedience is eternally damning. Parents teaching positive self-esteem without submission make it nearly impossible for their children to be used in the Kingdom. Parents spoiling children with the niceties of materialism without teaching selflessness only foster a selfish view. Parents showing wealth while never exemplifying sacrifice cause severe spiritual disadvantages. Many elders marvel at the intrinsic nature of this generation. However, children usually become what they have seen and heard from their parents.

It is ultimately the responsibility of a parent to enable the body of Christ by preparing the next generation for what God intends. Many adults proudly proclaim that God is going to pour out his Spirit upon all flesh in this hour. God is going to give a greater dimension of revival in this era than any other time in history. However, despite the beliefs, many live as though this will naturally occur. There is remarkably little preparation. Prayer has become a crutch the family pulls out in time of crisis. True sacrifice and commitment to God's purpose are increasingly absent. We've learned to live under the guise of faith while existing with a defeatist mentality. We don't want the world to influence our children, so we protect them to the point of natural suffocation. We prefer their biggest influences and relationships to remain within the walls of the home. We have forsaken the attitude of faith, for faith demands action in a world of compromise. We fear compromise so intently that we have abandoned the warfare mentality that has always defined faith. The commission to go into the world with the gospel of Jesus Christ should not be relegated to individuals. It should also include the family unit.

The greatest tragedy is that we are raising an army with conquered conceptualizations. Children do not just wake up one day magically equipped to handle the stress that comes with the call of God. They will not undertake some spiritual rite of passage that will endue them with the principles and power to be mightily used. Supernatural demonstration will not happen for those who are unprepared.

We are failing children in Kingdom preparedness. Most children and teenagers cannot even list the fruit of the Spirit. Many children can quote Acts 2:38 but know nothing about the gifts of the Spirit. They've heard about miracles, but most have never witnessed one. Where is the groundwork being laid in their lives for the last day move of God?

I am privileged to know families who do not just teach their children natural excellence. They also prepare them for the final evangelistic and apostolic thrust of God's power on this earth. Evangelists Steve and Shirley Carson, mentors and friends, live their lives in such a way. They encourage their son Stephen to excel in natural pursuits but have made it clear that God and His Kingdom are of absolute importance. They embrace ministry together, encourage Stephen in prayer and spiritual development, often asking him what he feels about spiritual matters and discerning of spirits in churches they are ministering in. Some may believe that it's dangerous to encourage a teenage boy to dabble in the gifts. However, Scripturally, spiritual training occurred remarkably early in the lives of children. God even bypassed a preoccupied prophet and spoke to a young child, Samuel. There's no doubt Stephen will be mightily used by God, because his parents impart anointing while demonstrating the means by which to attain it.

This is not to say that God bypasses all young people who do not have parents who instruct them, or that He uses all who do. However, living a humble life before God, consecrating to His purpose, submitting to His will, demonstrating compassion, and unconditionally loving others, will always get the attention of God. Devotion of this magnitude is most often imparted.

THE FAILURE OF INCONSISTENCY

Children are not ignorant. They are also remarkably observant. That is why it doesn't matter what parents instruct; children usually model what the parent lives instead of what they speak. One of the most detrimental sources a child ever learns from is the inconsistency of a parent. Many parents inadvertently teach that loyalty is voluntary, sacrifice optional, commitment conditional, and selflessness dispensable. Trying to reverse such ideas later adds confusion, because children know when parents' words and actions do not mesh. Teaching must go beyond theology and become authentic if it's going to take root in the hearts and minds of the youngest believers. If there is going to be a younger generation that arises to take the mantle of anointing and authority, there must be an elder generation that teaches the foundational principles and models the foundational values that God can build upon. If young people are going to create a legacy that extends into the next generation, they must have a foundation of real power, authority, and faith. In order to ensure a real experience continues, we must pass down a real experience to those under us.

The current generation must create more than hype, emotion, and exemplary programs. What this generation needs is a powerful, life-changing move of God. This move must begin in the home, not the church. Children learn from the way parents live, not from lessons taught at a place of worship. We cannot teach prayer, not pray, and expect kids to be spiritual. We cannot teach worship, not worship, and expect them to be worshippers. We cannot teach patience, kindness, and love, while possessing attitudes of negativity and continually judging one another. Doing this, while expecting kids to possess the attributes that are the fertile soil for God to penetrate and permeate, is impossible. We must live what we speak, or they will grow up to be even more inconsistent than we were.

THE BLANK SLATE

In a high school psychology class, I first learned the theory of the blank slate. Under this theory, humans have an empty cognitive center at birth. After birth, a person rapidly develops cognition through experiences. The more experience gained, the more knowledge that's also gained. The more knowledge a person obtains, the more they're ready for further experiences. This is a continual cycle throughout the lifespan. Man is forever learning, filling up the slate, until he dies.

Scripturally, we're not born with blank slates. Worse, man naturally lives under the degenerate power of a carnal nature as a slave to sin. Left alone, we could produce nothing but marred fruit leading to barren fields. This truth places the responsibility for establishing the culture necessary for the latter rain revival squarely on the shoulders of parents. The single greatest influence over a child's life, the authority that he cannot overcome, is the power wielded by a praying mom and dad.

Discipline is a must. Respect must be taught and re-enforced. Honesty and integrity must be instilled and guarded at all cost. Humility cannot be ignored. Selfishness must be recognized and removed. A child must learn that they cannot negatively behave as a means to get their way. Proper mannerisms consistent with both church and natural culture should be instilled. Christian parents should strive to make their children living, breathing, walking, and talking examples of Jesus Christ. Anything less than that goal is not acceptable. We're not born blank slates, but there are some blanks that must be filled in. Every parent should strive to ensure that the blanks are filled with Godly virtues not worldly vices.

God's view of the family's purpose in His kingdom is well above man's view. When God dealt with issues of the family, He wasn't attempting to bring a family together only in the natural sense. The family was not to be the strength that enabled an individual to bridge the gap between the temporal and eternal. The main source of power and encouragement for an individual was always intended to be God. A parent should teach their children that ultimate dependence is on God. Strength, power, love, and grace all flow from Him. Ultimately, His purpose is bigger than any family dynamic. His agenda should always take precedence.

In Luke 14, we read a particularly intriguing verse that seems to command a person to forsake family in order to become a disciple of Christ (verse 26). We should count the cost of any endeavor we undertake. We should know what we're getting ourselves into before we nonchalantly sell out for a cause. Many people read these verses and find excuse to enter monasteries.

However, Jesus did not desire to sever family relationships. He came to enhance family relationships and restore His perfect institution. What He wanted people to understand is that one cannot be a true disciple with anything in front of Kingdom purpose. The oft-missed principle is that the greatest service one can do for family is to place God first in it. If that is true, then the reciprocal is also true, the greatest injustice that one could do is claim Godly devotion but fail to put Him first in the family. If the family hears the talk of being a devoted Christian without seeing the sacrifice, commitment, vision, spirituality, faith, power, and anointing that comes with placing God's will above human will, we have failed.

Jesus was not only referring to counting the physical cost and making a determination to pay any price for the purpose of the Kingdom. The reverse lesson also had to be learned. Life is full of choices, and how we make those choices determines how it turns out. We're the byproduct of multiple decisions we've made.

There are two possible futures we're working to create. One is bright, while the other is undesirable. Every decision gravitates one toward either prospective outcome. Therefore, one must consider the burden on the family that may be caused by truly living for God. However, the gravest concern is what the family must pay if God is not placed as the first priority. What will it cost if we don't demonstrate holiness, discipleship, integrity, determination, commitment, love, and sacrifice. If our children don't see these Godly virtues in the home, where will they see them? Better yet, what will the world replace those Godly virtues with instead?

SATANIC TACTICS AGAINST FAMILY

The first satanic invasion against a natural creation wasn't leveled against man on an individual level. The first strike came against God's first and most sacred institution, the family. Even then, although not knowing why, the devil understood that there was something unique about the family that God had personally created.

The family structure is one of the most prolific examples of the relationship between God and man. A distorted view of marriage or the church presents a distorted view of the Father. Also, we learn that God considers His church to be a family unit, cohesively working together on His behalf. When one member of the church suffers, Christ said we should all suffer. When one member rejoices, He said we should all rejoice. We are to be that delicately linked in a larger family dynamic.

Careful analysis of Satan's attacks on the first family gives valuable insight into his current plans. He used his craftiness and cunning ability to lure Eve into a discussion of right and wrong that ultimately led to decision making. He tried to entice her with the redevelopment of lines that had been established to protect her. God had instructed Adam not to eat of the fruit. In turn, Adam instructed Eve not to eat it or touch it. He added an extra layer of protection to God's command. He broadened the boundaries to shield her from going against God's original law. The enemy's first attack was to trick her into foolishly reworking her boundaries.

Now is not the time for family compromise. The stakes are too high. Time is too short. The consequences are too broad. God established lines and set goals. He determined what consecrations had to be made. It's the job of every generation to try and understand why. However, it's not the job of each generation to undermine and weaken the protection handed down from prior generations. The moment Satan creates questions as to why the fruit cannot be touched, man inevitably questions why he cannot partake of it.

It's also crucial to notice that the Bible makes it clear that the sight of the tree stirred Eve (Genesis 3:6). This suggests that Eve had never seen the tree prior to the serpent's introduction. Adam had somehow isolated her from that part of the garden.

First of all, Eve began to debate the enemy on the necessity of what she'd obeyed since her creation. Eventually, this debate led her to check it out herself. However, authority has to be upheld. The man should follow God, and the woman should be submitted to her man. A family without the proper dynamics of submission is most vulnerable to spiritual attack, regardless of how involved they are in the church's functionality.

Children must witness submission exemplified in the life of their parents. It must be mutual and equally displayed. The husband gets respect, not because he demands it, but because he loves his wife and acts as the spiritual leader of the home. The wife's emotional needs are met, not because she complains, but because she's submitted and a true helpmate to her husband.

True submission is not an action. It is an attitude that requires action. It's a humble willingness to submit to God, His precepts, and conditions. This powerful dimension is missing in many of today's churches because parents do not reinforce it in the home. That's the way the enemy attacks. While we wage war on homosexuality, sex, ungodly apparel, and drugs; Far too often, we ignore the way these large sins quietly intrude into family life. We forget that a fall usually begins with attitudes of negativism, rejection, selfishness, and rebellion. We must guard against the silent enemy seeking to perpetrate the home.

THE RESPONSIBILITY OF A MAN

Women are essential to God. That's an excellent place to start, for many religious men still live under the misguided assumption that women are inferior. Woman is to be subjected to man. She's the "lesser" creature. Therefore, she should take a backseat to man's egocentric lifestyle. That's simply not true, and any man living as such is out of line with God's will.

The lesser creature merely refers to physical strength and emotional stability. A man only merits the respect of being "greater" when he loves the "lesser" how God intended. If he doesn't fulfill this basic need, he's deserving of nothing.

Left alone, man has always been a poor image of God. Observe only the traditional strength and rational thought of man and vast parts of the God story are missing. However, combine the nurturing instincts and emotional involvement of a woman with the hard and deliberate nature of man and the distorted image of God becomes clear. God knew that Adam was incomplete and decided that the missing component was a woman. He created the perfect blend to mesh with man's disposition. God is only properly viewed by examining both natures.

God values women tremendously. It's difficult to view women properly in a culture that downgrades them at every opportunity. Pornography is despicable because it not only devalues the woman involved, it undermines the respect and innocence that God intended women to have. Women were never intended to be an object of man's desires. She was never supposed to be unimportant and insignificant except to fulfill some lustful act in a bedroom.

God created the woman to assist the man. It's simply un-Godly to claim to be a man of integrity, a minister, or someone Kingdom-minded while engaging in activities that devalue women. However, many ministers addict themselves to pornography. This greatly limits the apostolic authority that God would give and may literally lead to spiritual bondage and oppression.

Notice the words God used. Man must "honor the weaker vessel." God did not say to honor the weak vessel. This distinction is significant because God highlighted that there's no delineation of strong and weak. Male or female, we're all weak vessels. The woman is merely the weaker of the two. Man must not prop himself up and pretend to be in control.

Control is an illusion. No one has the power to decide what happens tomorrow. We're never in control and are always subject to the will and ways of God. Pride gets in the way, but everyone desperately needs God's love and compassion to permeate their life. Only then can we become the people that God intended.

Another weakness exploited by Satan was Adam's lack of spiritual discernment. Adam took the proper natural steps to protect Eve. He drew lines that were even more preventative than the ones God had given him. Adam valued Eve, or he wouldn't have tried to shield her from a danger he didn't fully understand. However, his effort to protect her with more rules failed.

Far too many Christian fathers make the same mistake today. To think that the rules and combined traditions of religion will protect children is ridiculous. The belief that training substitutes for spiritual awareness is foolish. It's still the responsibility of man to be the priest of the home, the sentinel on the wall, the strongman, and protector of the family unit. Most men would die to protect their family from physical harm. However, most are far less concerned about issues of eternal significance. One must do more to discern the family's spirituality in context with God's will for each member that he's been given care over.

By all Scriptural indication, Adam was standing near as Eve ate the fruit. He was there but too preoccupied with his own life that he failed to notice until it was too late. One of the greatest charges leveled against today's fathers is to be physically present, but emotionally and spiritually absent.

It's the father's responsibility, not just his right, to know who his children are hanging around, how they are spending their time, where they are spending money, what they are watching and listening to, and who they are texting, IMing, emailing, and Facebooking. Fathers who allow their children to idolize secular icons are setting their children up for disaster. Parents who try to add spiritual virtues to worldly role models are building on a faulty foundation. Men must aggressively remove the world's influence from their homes.

It's the man's responsibility to know what's going on in his wife's world. The moment a man devalues his own convictions and allows his spouse to take headship, even in a symbolic way, he undermines God's order of submission. Once that chain breaks, it is hard to re-establish, and the family is open to satanic influence and worldly involvement. He should love his wife, letting her know how beautiful and special she is, for as the old adage states, "if he doesn't, another man will."

Even if the wife is too strong to fall to Satan's snare in a sexual way, a true husband will leave no room for his wife to feel insecure, lonely, afraid, or uncertain of the future. She should be safe in knowing that her fate is tied to the hands of a praying man.

It's the man's responsibility to draw lines around his family that cannot be crossed externally or internally. He should protect his family at all cost, regardless of who is offended or doesn't agree. If he senses the slightest hint of danger, he should do everything in his power to keep those under his charge protected. Everyone in the family may not understand every line. They don't even have to agree with every line. However, it's man's responsibility to make sure that the family honors every line. Honoring the lines protects from the deception of sin that's always crouching at the door.

Adam also failed in that he ate the fruit after Eve did. What would have happened to Adam had he not eaten the fruit? The first covenant relationship was between God and Adam. God never personally instructed Eve. What would have happened had Adam scolded Eve, but kept the original covenant? We'll never know.

God stepped into the chaos man created and spoke, not to Eve but to the man. We consider Eve the more guilty party, but God placed Eve in a secondary role. He made Adam the primary subject of His investigation.

"Adam, where art thou?"

Adam followed the temptation born of selfishness that so many of us follow. He immediately blamed both God and the woman for his role in eating the fruit. He refused to be held accountable for his own actions. In his mind, everyone else was at fault for the derailment of his domestic tranquility. The problem was that he created an atmosphere of disunity that caused the severest of fissures in their relationship. Most Christian marriages end up exactly the same way the moment we minimize God. It's not only what we're bringing into the home that creates the rift into secularism. At times, it's what we're unknowingly pushing out of the home that causes the breach. We cannot diminish God and maintain the same level of power and anointing. Building a family on anything other than an effective relationship with God and His immutable Word is far too dangerous. As God walks out the door, so does the hope of the family.

AS MAN GOES

After everything had transpired in the garden, and the curses had been verbally handed down, an angel with a flaming sword stepped to the entrance. He brought a momentary mission and memorable message. His purpose was to drive a desperate Adam from Eden, forever expelling him from paradise. The wording is powerfully revelatory.

The angel drove out the man.

The established message is that as a man goes, so goes the family. The angel specifically drove Adam from the place God had established. He paid no attention to Eve, for an eternal principle was being established. Precedence was being set. The husband is responsible for the protection and spiritual stability of the family. As the husband goes, so do those under him.

This places a heavy burden on the shoulders of Christian men to step up and become more consecrated to God and more separated from the world. God chose this as the reality of life because He uses the relationship between a man and his wife to exemplify the relationship between He and His church. The first Adam ate of the fruit and died [with] his bride. The second Adam died [for] His bride. Therefore, we are to live for God first, especially within the family.

The family is the basic building block of the church. Since that's the case, the family is also the fundamental unit of the Kingdom. That fact cannot be ignored. God expects families to be involved in His business. We're only as safe as we condition our families to be. We must never forget the importance of family.

CONCLUSION

There's an attack on the family that is both natural and spiritual in nature. Demonic forces seek to destroy the home at all cost. The view, through the effects of Hollywood and other entertainment methods, is disheartening. The casual attitude that most Americans have toward marriage and its longevity is disturbing. The plummeting nature of the political landscape concerning the family is spiritually appalling. However, these are only clear reminders of the invisible attacks being launched in the spirit realm. The natural world mirrors the celestial, and in the natural, the basic family unit has never been so antagonized, devalued, and mocked.

If the church is going to survive the onslaught of hell's hounds and live above the influence of secular America, it must do more than create mantras to live by. It must do more than spend quality time together. Men must remember that we're not fighting flesh and blood. Ultimately, this is spiritual. Fathers must establish a system of submission in the home. He must become unwavering in his personal commitment and family's continued efforts to reach God and others. If true submission is not achieved, the family fights a losing battle.

Despite the bleak outlook, all hope is not lost. God still values the family, and what God values, He protects. As soon as a family becomes established on God's Word and Spirit, an anointing comes that causes the family to soar above the effects of this world. When the family aligns with God's purpose, apostolic power will follow.

May every family reading these words be blessed and do whatever it takes to move into a deeper dimension in Christ. Amen.

Prisons With Stained Glass Windows

9
PROBLEMS, PASSION, AND PURPOSE

There's no component of Christian living as detrimental or advantageous as passion. That's the reason the enemy has become so obsessive about stealing all enthusiasm from the people of God. The enemy wants to fight a depressed people. He delights in dealing with the oppressed, frustrated, and weary. He loves destroying the downcast and weak. Satan has learned that a people with a defeated mentality never possess the apostolic power that defeats him.

The true body of Christ is not feeble or defeated. It's still vibrant, healthy, and unafraid of the devil, even while staring the corruption of the world and the overwhelming forceful spirit of this age in the face.

There's never been an era when the people of God have

been so downtrodden. Joy is a rare commodity in the majority of Christian homes. True peace is a pipe dream, one that most believers have almost given up. Occasional happiness gives most Christians hope to continue fighting another day, even if the mountaintops are ever fleeting and another war waits on the other side. If we're not careful, we give in to the tide of disillusionment that attempts to overwhelm us, believing that all there will be until God returns is fighting, famine, and frustration. Living in the grip of negative emotions, we never firmly grasp the notion that God has called a people to be separated from the dregs of the defeated to become a powerful army.

. . . . . .

The young man ran through the cavernous darkness. His heart pounded in his chest until he thought it would explode. He was running from an enemy that he couldn't see for the dimness surrounding him. At this point, he was much too tired to be afraid.

He paused for a moment, stopping to listen to the sounds that should've been echoing through the rocky corridors if his pursuers were still giving chase. Yet, as he stood in the shadows, all he heard was the faint beating in his own chest and a stream running off a stone ledge in the distance.

He started again and walked for what seemed like hours. He moved deeper into the caves, making sure that it would be almost impossible to track him.

His small frame was not one that most men would be

ashamed of. His skin was drawn taut over muscles that somewhat bulged under his coat. The tiredness in his face and fatigue in his posture did nothing to hide his boyish good looks. The elements couldn't hide his stately appearance.

Finally, he found what he was looking for, a small opening just large enough for a child. However, he contorted his way through the maze of stony crevices until he reached the other side. As he passed through, he knew he was almost to his destination.

A few minutes later, he saw the faint glow of a familiar fire dancing across a shadowy ledge of sandstone. His senses were at ease. He was almost home.

However, as he approached, a faint sound in the trees to his left alarmed him. He slowed then, angling himself in that direction in case an attack should come. His sword was pulled two-thirds from its scabbard, ready to strike a fatal blow if necessary. He'd always hoped it wouldn't come to that, but he'd killed before. It was how he'd become known. He was a famous killer, a renowned man of war.

A noise to his right echoed louder than the first. He shifted his gait further to the left, inching away from the newest sound. However, he heard the soft rustling of a branch in that direction too. It was barely audible, but it had been there.

Normally, it would have meant nothing more than the wind or perhaps a small animal scurrying through the trees. However, today it meant something different, for that sound was particularly distinct. He'd heard the easily recognizable sound of a tree branch rubbing against cloth. There was no mistaking it... At least two men were in the trees around him.

He quickly thought through the possibilities. The most logical attack point was the area in front where trees merged into one pathway. If they were going to move on him, that would be the place.

He didn't want to walk into a well-laid ambush. So, he unexpectedly drew his sword, quickly charging toward the right. Two men sprang out with swords drawn, and another charged swiftly from the left.

He was no stranger to warfare. He'd started off just an ordinary shepherd, but that had been another lifetime ago. Now, he was a seasoned soldier, benefiting from years on the run for crimes he wasn't guilty of.

His muscles tensed as they normally did, but there was no real nervousness. This was all too common. He trusted, from years of experience, that this was another threat that would be swiftly eradicated. God hadn't brought him this far to abandon him.

He slowly pivoted his body forward as the men began to circle. The moonlight glistened off his polished blade. It was comforting to know that it was as sharp as it was shiny.

The three men didn't appear afraid either. They'd obviously been in dangerous situations before as well. The lone stranger reached onto his head with his free hand, slowly removing the hood he'd been wearing to keep his identity unknown from his earlier pursuers. As the hood fell, one of the three men spoke,

"David? Sir, is that you?"

Still holding his sword at the ready, the loner replied with a simple nod. One by one the three men walked closer, each man lowering his weapon. The suspense that had been hanging in the atmosphere was replaced with a warmth not expected moments earlier. Laughter filled the night air as the men welcomed David home.

"We've missed you, brother. You've been gone a few days. We were starting to grow concerned," one whispered.

One patted David on the back, "I thought we were going to have to come down and get you, sir. We would've killed them all."

David chuckled lightly. These men were loyal and would do everything in their power to protect him. "Kill them all," David thought as he smiled. They would have too.

The imagery of David and the mighty army that were raised from the rejects has never been more relevant. He led men who had lost families, lost land, taken lives, been accused of crimes, been abandoned as failures, hidden in fear, and been taken advantage of in malicious ways. Most of them didn't fight for honor or family pride. They'd fought only to protect themselves from a society that had rejected them. They'd fought to remain isolated from a world they'd chosen to flee. Collectively, they'd felt that their lives were better served wallowing in the shame of their own regrets.

That's how they'd lived emotionally, until David had

shown up. This small, retired shepherd had challenged their meager existence. He'd stirred feelings that had long since been buried. What they'd felt from him wasn't more of the same mediocrity they'd grown accustomed to. When he spoke to them, they were overwhelmed with a sense of hope. He didn't incite riot or speak in negligent manners about the kingdom of the sinful Saul who'd been trying to kill him.

Rather, David chose to deal in the positive aspects of life, restoring order and peace to the chaos they'd established. He was fair, honest, and reasonable. They'd heard of his countenance. They'd even heard the horror stories from Philistine campfires. They'd intently listened to the rumors of a soldier who would kill anyone who stood in his path. The one who would come and restore order to the kingdom that had been dishonored and disgraced by the current regime.

Since he'd joined them, they'd found that all these rumors had not been accurate. David was everything they'd ever imagined and more. He'd won their hearts and earned their respect, turning them from the lowest motley crew in Israel, to one of the most feared armies on the planet.

As God scans the natural confines of the earth from the celestial grandeur of Heaven, He diligently desires to find an army rising from the deepest entanglements of emotional and physical dilemma. However, what He often encounters is a people still stuck in the mire of fundamental religion, which has no power to deliver from the oppression and guilt of sin. He finds people so trapped in the snares of their own carnality that they can't view the hope and peace in His hands.

Far too many Christians feel that living for God is too difficult. A wise man of God once told me, no doubt echoing the words of many who'd gone before him,

"Boy, if you live for God hard, it'll be easy. However, if you live for God easy, it'll be hard."

From the age of 13, I've never forgotten those words. More than once, that wise message has proven true. If one wants to do more than survive in this era of commercialism, false religion, and humanism, one must live for God with true passion. If a hunger for more of God, to truly be intimate with Jesus Christ isn't ever present in one's life, the fervency for which one lives will usually dwindle as the battle wages and the pressure rises. We must learn to fall in love with Christ, bringing with us the passion of His love. He must become the object of our obsession.

OBSESSION

She'd been raised with her brother, a cunning, crafty deceiver and opportunist always looking to sham someone for personal gain. Living in Mesopotamia, under the old Babylonian mentality and self-pleasing principles, hadn't been easy. She'd grown up in the land that Abraham had fled from in order to fulfill God's plan many years prior. She'd always known this wasn't the best place to begin, if one wanted to do something renowned for the Kingdom of God.

However, she was born with divine destiny inside of her. She'd always known she was different from other girls. She'd never developed the same selfish motivations as most of her peers. However, even she didn't know the enormous potential and providence that was inside of her. She was going to become a mother in the genealogy of God's chosen people.

She'd never understood the reason she didn't fit in with the crowd. She'd never known why her thoughts were so different. She couldn't see that the rejection and awkwardness of friends and family was molding her into something special. She was being shaped into a shining star that would be elevated from her mediocre life and thrust into the opportunity of a lifetime at just the right moment. Her life changed climactically, the moment she first met and held the gaze of the wealthy and handsome man named Isaac.

Rebekah walked to meet Isaac with a stranger, for how can one embrace destiny without risks? How can one embark on an epic adventure without persisting through the adversity of an unsure beginning?

Rebekah was Isaac's comforter at the death of his mother, for there's always suffering on the journey toward the will of God. How can one survive if loss is not embraced as part of the journey just as much as gain?

Years later, Rebekah was responsible for Jacob obtaining the blessing from Isaac. She's often cast in a bad light for her role in the deception, but she'd never forgotten the prophecy foretelling that her younger son would rule her elder. She knew that two nations had struggled in her womb. She'd been given a glimpse into God's plan, and she was willing to take risks in order to propel the promise into fulfillment.

It's also Rebecca who recognized Jacob's potential and tapped into his desire and determination for greater things. Rebekah also noticed that the girls in the area often sidetracked him. Therefore, she convinced Isaac to send him away, so his ultimate purpose wouldn't be denied. She sacrificed her closeness with her favored son, surrendering her motherly instinct to protect him. It's ultimately Rebekah who stands in the annals of history with God in support of Jacob, despite the fact that Esau was the rightful heir. Rebekah understood the relationship between passion, potential, and purpose.

Rebekah teaches modern Christianity a lesson about fulfilling destiny. It's far too easy to become casual when we're unsure what God desires. We drift toward stagnation and complacency when God's divine directive has not been clearly communicated. The principal threat is that apathy is the worst place to reside if one desires to be fixed firmly into God's plan. Destiny doesn't come to the idle, those stuck in a secular state of neutrality. It doesn't find those transfixed in futile and frustrated emotions, doubting if God will ever show up. Destiny always comes to those with a heart of passion.

Despite modern attempts to obscure the truth from those called by God, destiny isn't something one must search for. One is born with divine destiny. God designed everyone with intent. He placed the right mixture of pedigree, promise, potential, and personality into each of us. We're able to accomplish extraordinary things if we face each task head on, because God has supernaturally equipped us with everything we need to accomplish what He created us for.

However, with that understanding still comes the knowledge that one doesn't just trip on the road of life and fall into divine destiny. One never just accidentally discovers a miracle. It's impossible to slip on one of life's proverbial banana peels, hit your head on the ground, knock yourself out, and wake up in the land of fulfillment. There's no such thing as passive Christianity. It always battles, climbs, digs, and meets needs. A passionless Pentecost is a powerless Pentecost. There's a mutual relationship, a collaborative effort that must exist to ensure that one becomes what they were designed to become. If one desires to be more than a casual Christian with minimal kingdom influence, he or she must accept responsibility for ensuring that the anointing goes from implantation to completion.

The greatest barrier that must be overcome on the path to fulfilling apostolic destiny is to understand the gap that exists between the promise of God and the performance of God. At times, everyone doubts God's desire to complete what He started. In those moments of misery, the enemy attempts to destroy the fervor with which the struggling believer lives for God. If he can steal your passion, he causes you to become passive, destroying your effectiveness for the Kingdom.

The confused Christian searches for answers to resolve the conflicting emotions that arise. However, during times of searching, we must become more unified of purpose. If we'll align ourselves with God's Kingdom purpose, He'll take care of the rest. If we're passionate about the things He's passionate about, God will keep us in His divine will.

Manipulation isn't necessary when one aligns with God's

agenda. Political posturing isn't necessary when promoting God's plan first. Natural management isn't needed when faith is placed in an unfailing God. In His omniscience, God has already orchestrated eternity to line itself with your destiny. The steps of a righteous man are ordered of the Lord. Every negative feedback, every doubter along the way, every mistake, misfortune, missed opportunity, and failure, God utilizes to create something noteworthy. He uses difficulties to conform you into a vessel of honor for apostolic outpouring.

God is frustrated with contemporary Christianity and Pentecostalism proclaiming His name but refusing to engage in His kingdom. It's easier to serve Him like statues in dulling cathedrals than to actively engage in His purpose.

The greatest tragedy of those who have partaken in the life changing Pentecostal experience is an indifferent attitude toward God. While frequently encountering the presence of the most dangerous, powerful, majestic, exciting, explosive, perfect, righteous, holy, life changing, and eternal God, we calmly coexist with Him. Dangerously, we become calloused, cold, and passionless.

The enemy attempts to destroy this generation's church with spiritual laziness and lack of commitment to Godly living. It's not that we're lazy in general. It's not that we lack passion. It's not that we lack conviction. It's not even that we lack excitement. The reality is that we possess all of those attributes, we just carelessly place them in the wrong areas of life. Most of us are passionate about something. We must make sure that our greatest passion is about Jesus.

Somewhere along the way, many have missed it. God no longer enamors, terrifies, or amazes His church. Encountering the All-righteous has become ritual. Christ the Creator has become common, the Sacred has become secondary to other priorities of life. The miraculous has become nothing more than mildly anticipated. Time spent with the Majestic is mundane and mediocre. Where is the passion?

Passion always supersedes performance. How far one goes in his walk with God will ultimately be determined by the veracity with which he attacks his task. Passion is always more foreshadowing than predictions. Prophecy without passion seldom becomes reality. Passion always precedes divine promotion. God will not advance those who aren't passionate about glorifying Him. Passion always indicates pretense. One will always know where a person's true loyalties lie by examining what they're most passionately pursuing. Passion is always precursory to potential. Again, where is the passion?

PASSION AND PERSONALITY

There's a definite glitch in the church that causes some to feel that they're inadequate at reaching people for the Kingdom of God. Some have utilized terminology that's not Biblical and misleads the masses, causing only a few to become involved in God's main Kingdom purpose.

The term "soul winner" has been liberally applied to people who "win souls" (which is a Biblical principle). He that winneth souls is wise (Proverbs 11:30). However, the context in which Solomon wrote, gives an indication as to its purpose. One should be wise to win souls. Winning souls is more about "how to" than "have to." To serve the purpose of God on this earth, one must learn how to commit to a lifestyle of loving others.

Outreach terminology scares many people from reaching the lost because they feel they must have a certain personality. This is far from God's truth. God mightily used people of all personality types in His Word, and they were all equally important. They complement each other to accomplish a common Godly purpose. God used deep thinkers who plotted and planned before action, as well as spontaneous men who lived from moment to moment. He used pushy and bossy types just as often as the non-confrontational. He used people who were uncomfortable being who they were, and those who had grown accustomed to using their God given strengths to compliment the Kingdom.

The gravest mistake that well-meaning but misguided Christians make is in attempting to live outside of their talents and gifting in order to complete the Kingdom. However, this violates the sheer nature of God. One cannot be everything the Kingdom needs. If that were possible, one would be devoured by pride, devastating both himself and the Kingdom. It's true that one should strive to be better. We should work to reinforce our strengths, spending the majority of our time focusing on what we can do.

Perfecting each type of personality flaws within is impossible and comes close to playing God. Paul was intelligent enough to grasp this principle when he declared,

"I have planted, Apollos watered, but God gave the increase (1 Corinthians 3:6).

There are diversities of gifts, diversities of personalities, diversities of offices, and diversities of anointing for a reason. God demands unity. No one is successful without the rest. No man is an island. No one can stand alone. We all need God, and we all need each other. Passion overshadows personality.

THE THEOLOGY OF A SMILE

The long faces found on most Christians are a sad testimony as to the goodness of God. Once, when working as an audiologist at an otolaryngologist's office, I came to work sick. The doctor called me into his office when he saw I was sweating from fever and had been coughing all morning. He thanked me for being willing to work through sickness, but then jokingly made the statement,

"Jonathan, you're bad advertisement right now."

Being a doctor, he was aware that my sickness took away from his credibility at the moment. I wonder how God feels, surrounded by people who claim to be full of His love, goodness, and peace, yet never smile. The power of a smile goes a long way, as does the power of a frown. Kindness cannot be demonstrated through a scowl. Love is not best shown through looks of contempt. Healing is not best advertised from people who are never pleased. We must learn to smile and allow others to see God's grace and perfection radiating. After all, if we believe what we say, we have much to be thankful for.

LOVE IS ABOUT LOSING

There's nothing more compelling and powerful, yet more misunderstood than the concept of love. There are many definitions provided by philosophers, poets, songwriters, movie producers, and romantics suggesting that the reality of love is a misrepresented notion. No one knows just how to define love in the 21st century. The lines that once defined an idea of such complexity have been eradicated by erroneous views. The deterioration of concepts that always made love easily discernible have altered the landscape of emotional stability, creating a crisis concerning the definition of love.

However, despite the intricacy of this subject and the varying opinions in modern philosophy, one thing is not debatable. Every human being is in dire need of love. It's difficult to survive alone in this modern era. Advancements in communication have bridged gaps that in prior years were impossible. Contact is at the push of a button. Connection is at a fingertip. Facebook and other social networks have made relationships an easy goal to achieve.

The problem with this is that relationships continually grow less personal and even less committed than at any other time in history. Man's constructs of love have decidedly dimmed. We stand to lose the passion and commitment we've always had to God, because culture tells us that less is more. We can still have intimacy without the time it takes to nurture and grow real love.

This trend hasn't developed without repercussions. Lack of true intimacy with others, and more importantly with God, has resulted in an emotional collapse. Suicide and depression are at an all time high. Mental health issues are a significant concern in the United States. There's more loneliness, isolation, stress, and compulsive disorders diagnosed today than at any other time in history. It seems that Christians feel more isolated the more "connected" they become.

Cultural connectivity has done nothing to make people feel more accepted, validated, and loved. However, that's the one thing people are in steady search of. They want to be valued the way they are.

I was playing in the backyard with my son, Hudson, when God began to deal with me. Hudson had been "racing" me all afternoon, and I had failed to win one race, although I was much faster than a five-year-old. God spoke to me, "Love is about losing."

It's the innate nature of a man to want to win. From the time I was old enough to compete, I had no desire to finish second. As a young child, this nature was so severe that I often cheated to prevail. I've watched the competitive nature in my own two sons, and smiled remembering what it was like to have those feelings. Grown men playing basketball or volleyball at the church's activity center exhibit no less testosterone, as the deep craving for dominance lives in most of us.

However, there I was, "losing" many times to a toddler. The truth stormed into my spirit with a force that almost overwhelmed me. When one truly loves, he or she doesn't mind losing. Pride and politics are no longer pertinent. Love determines that it's not about me anymore. It's all about the one my heart belongs to.

Any father who dominates His children and refuses to allow them the positive emotion of winning isn't fit to be a father. Likewise, any Christian living selfishly outside of God's purpose, while passionately pursuing his or her own desires, doesn't truly display God's love. Believers who have never gotten over themselves, who cannot truly live for God and others first, have not moved beyond the base level of Christianity. The love of God was always intended to flow outward. God's people were always supposed to know that love is about losing.

. . . .

He was much too young to die. It was never supposed to happen like this. He'd been his mother's pride, his father's promise, his people's hope for a brighter future. He'd lived an obedient life, always understanding that somehow God had ambitious plans on using him for a greater purpose. He'd done everything to align himself with the will and purpose of God. His heart was pure, his mind at ease, and his garments spotless. He was a loving son who would one day be a devoted father.

Although, the odds of that seemed remarkably slim in this moment. He'd been bound and placed on a table of stone. It was like a scene unveiling from the pagan rituals he'd heard concerning the barbarians in Babylon. He could imagine the flowing blood from the sharp instrument piercing the flesh. He could almost see the laughing and mockery from onlookers around pagan temples, as they offered another sacrifice to evil gods who'd probably never existed. However, they continued killing in order to gain divine providence and protection. What a waste it all seemed, but here he was. It appeared that his fate would be the same as those ridiculously sacrificed on barren altars.

He couldn't push the questions from his mind. How could this be happening? Only yesterday, he'd been dreaming of standing with his father and pursuing God together. He wondered how this would affect the man he knew loved him more than life. As he thought of his mother, tears flooded his eyes. She would be expecting them home soon, and he probably never would see her again. If he would've only known what was going to take place today, he would've told her yesterday how much she mattered. He would give anything to hold her one more time, to tell her how he loved her for all she'd poured into his life. He knew that would never happen. He was here, tied down, hopelessly empty, and ready to be offered.

He looked into the sunlight, and squinted to look into his killer's eyes. Fear engulfed him, as he saw the unmistakable glare of bright reflection on a blade, as the dagger raised swiftly into the air. Their eyes locked for just a moment, murderer and victim, executioner and condemned, killer and prey, father and son.

Isaac took one last breath, closing his eyelids, trying to stop the confusion in his mind. It was true that he'd laid himself on this altar. Not fully understanding what was taking place, he'd been willing to sacrifice everything. He wasn't fully aware of his purpose in God's holy agenda. He couldn't altogether trust that aspect of what he was going through. However, the one thing he did trust was that Abraham knew the voice of God. If Abraham said he was doing God's will, Isaac wasn't going to stop him. In a final act of loyalty that seems to transcend human reason, he was willing to offer his life as an ultimate sacrifice. Love was about losing.

Two men left that mountaintop forever changed. Abraham learned that he could trust God but so did Isaac. He also learned that no price was too high if God asked it of a man. Both men knew that God was first in each of their lives, regardless of what had to be given along the journey. Both men had a newfound respect for each other, for both had looked into the other's eyes at the greatest challenge of their lives, and each had recognized total abandonment and surrender to the plan of God. Son not knowing why his life had to be taken, and father not understanding why he was asked to murder his child, but both willing to play their parts in the story that God had orchestrated. God longs for men and women who'll serve him today with that same level of devotion and commitment.

> **The true test of love is how one responds when God is silent.**

However, today's cultural feelings are much more frigid toward sacrifice. It's easy to serve God when the seas are smooth. It's an indictment against the nature of human love when we love God only when He works for us. The true test of love is how we respond when God is silent.

How do we react with tattered sails, and the boisterous winds cause aimless drifting through stormy seas? When sorrow and sickness overtake us, the enemy mocks at our calamity, and we have more questions than answers, how much love do we demonstrate then? When there's no affirmation and no feeling of appreciation, where's the love then? When life destroys, dampens, and depresses, we must remember that sometimes unfortunate things happen in the will of God.

Paul knew what it was like to go through the rough waters of life. He'd been shipwrecked on multiple occasions, thrown in prison many times, and left for dead outside of Lystra. He was lost on an island with barbaric strangers. A poisonous viper bit him as he was trying to build a fire. He spent most of his adult life running from mad Christians whose only desire was to kill him. However, it is Paul who penned the now famous words.

"I am persuaded..."

In spite of everything he'd encountered, Paul still stated, "I'm convinced, certain, sure, convicted, confident, that nothing can separate me from the love of God."

He understood that life would be full of failure, struggles, mishaps, misfortunes, missed opportunities, and imperfections. However, true love isn't concerned with losses, because true love never fails.

From man's limited perspective, we often feel that God has abandoned us in times of darkest struggle and need. We often feel that we've slipped into the judgments of God. That must be the reason for difficult trails. However, when one has lived to the best of their ability, continually reaching toward greater intimacy with God, it's rarely judgment that moves one into the hard areas of life. Most often, believers are ushered into deeper conflicts by love.

Love offers losses instead of wins. Most often, it's blood, sweat, and tears on which we build the dreams most sacred. Bliss is engulfed in trials. Healing is enveloped in sickness. The enemy always offers an easy way out, as both sides of eternity earnestly wonder if we'll cave to the temptation or continue walking toward enlightenment. These are the moments when God attempts to draw us nearer.

However, if we're not careful, we'll walk away and never realize that God was repositioning us for power, enabling us to perform his kingdom business. Usually, when looking at the people most anointed and highly used in the deeper avenues of God's Spirit, if observing more closely, one can see the scars not quite healed from battles that brought the depth that determined their greatness. Do not ignore those scars, just ask Jesus. He carries them too, for love is about losing.

COUNTERING GUILT

The enemy often uses guilt from previous mistakes against new converts. The church must be better aware of this tactic and must prepare a response. The absolute worst response from a church member is to see a new baby in God and judge them for mistakes. If a child is spanked for falling off of his bike the first time he tries to ride without the aid of training wheels, there's a problem in the heart of the parent. However, this is the way that many "saints" attempt to develop those who are brand new to the godliness.

Instead, the church must be watchful for chances to display the love, patience, and grace of God. When a new convert fails, and they will, the church must be there to pick them up and gently place them back on the right pathway. By truly displaying grace, the church teaches the convert how to love God and how to accept God's favor. These lessons far outweigh what they'll learn about judgment and fear otherwise. The church should almost overcompensate to love someone who's in need of grace. As Mother Theresa stated, "A person needs love most when they deserve love least."

Many times well meaning church members send unintended messages to new converts, often messages of doubt and lack of acceptance. All though the purpose of discussion may have been to encourage the new convert toward the path of holiness more quickly, the unintended message speaks louder than the actual words used.

When an established saint attempts to pastor a new convert, it demonstrates impatience concerning the personal journey the convert is on. Impatience unintentionally indicates mistrust, lack of faith, or fear.

On the other-hand, the patient approach, letting the new convert know that you are proud of any changes they have made speaks the opposite. It convinces the convert that they can change and demonstrates how much faith the believer has in what God can work in a person's life. We must learn to exercise patience in helping others overcome guilt and adjust to a holy lifestyle.

THE WILL OF GOD

There's an imminent danger lurking around every corner for those who have sensed the call of God and are responding to that call. This threat doesn't violently impose itself on the will of believers by sheer force. The enemy is simply not that strong. The peril is often presented expertly, intricately woven into the very fabric of what it means to be called. Hell doesn't care if a believer is a casual observer of the deeper ministry of the Holy Ghost, as long as he or she doesn't become involved. Watching is a necessary evil that the enemy must allow for, if the believer is to be deceived into thinking they are truly apostolic. However, participation is strictly forbidden, for if one participates, he or she will recognize that there's no limit to what God will do.

What has always set men and women who have been mightily used of God apart is the way they engage the Kingdom. Some attempt to live for God on their own terms, continuing to build fleshly empires, while struggling to let His legacy overshadow their own. However, the truly successful in the Kingdom have long since relinquished control of their lives to a much higher purpose, recognizing that self is lost in the grand aura of God.

Moses was one such person. Scripture reveals, "God made known His ways unto Moses, His acts unto the children of Israel," (Psalm 103:7). Moses recognized on a grand scale that there was a vast difference between the glory of God and the omnipresence of God. The people were content to murmur about seeing the handiwork of God but never experienced Him intimately. Moses found it much harder to complain because of a desire to not only witness but also walk with God. That yearning led him past the others who were content to dream of better days. It led him to a cleft in the rock experience that resulted in him seeing the aura of God's presence. It wasn't even the physical sight of the Lord he'd discerned, just a changing in the atmosphere, but it moved him beyond the normal limitations of humanity and intensified his obsession with the Almighty. The people were content to stop with signs and natural manifestations of God's presence, but Moses needed more. He profoundly desired to be a vessel that God used to demonstrate His glory and power on the earth.

Today, the issue hasn't changed. Apostolic power and authority comes to those who are committed and consecrated to developing an inner desire that propels them into a deeper relationship with God. To them, the cross has not been reduced to a symbol without substance. They fully recognize prior sacrifices, and understand that true believers glory in their own weakness, while sharing in Christ's suffering. They haven't selected ministry for comfort but calling, ever ready to pay the price to pursue their uncertain future in His unending story. They aren't moved by hardship, for they know that struggle is the breeding ground of anointing. The battle is the birthing place of apostolic ministry.

There has never been a man or woman of God who didn't endure the hardship of struggle between the grips of two worlds. The natural world promising that life could be easier if all supernatural concepts are surrendered. The eternal world promising a way of escape and a lesson through every trial. Every one who has ever been highly favored and chosen had to endure the struggle of birthing a burden. The bitter tears, agonizing loneliness, feelings of being forgotten, loss of self, pain of losing pertinence to the world, vulnerability, and lapse of human strength make the transition into the Spirit realm awkward for humans. However, it's necessary. The presence of God is revealed during personal moments of uncomfortable intimacy. Man discovers the God He loves, and God reveals more with each new level of relationship. We need a private cleft in the rock experience that can only come through becoming personal with Jesus.

One of the trademarks of 21st century Christianity is the way in which we unashamedly worship God. This is one area that must never change. However, we often lack understanding of what worship truly is. It isn't just a visible demonstration of excitement about God's worthiness. True worship isn't grounded in emotionalism. It's emotional, but it's not an emotional response at the core. True worship is a humble reverence, a lifting of God to the forefront of human existence. It's paying homage to the Creator of the universe.

> **Worship means to recognize who we're not, inside the grandeur of who He is.**

If worship is lifting God up for who He is, how can we truly worship God deeply without a progressive revelation of Him? If connection with God is severed to the point that He's not exposing Himself in a personal way, we're incapable of real worship. By this definition, worship is more a lifestyle than an action rendered in a Sunday service. True worship is born from having the curtain pulled back and clearly viewing eternal principles. This only occurs after one personally walks away from those centered only on modern Christian views.

God longs for those who walk past religion and into relationship, passing those paralyzed in the pilgrimage of fundamentalism. He longs for those intimate moments where man strips away the priestly garments to kneel in sackcloth and ashes, remembering the lowliness of humanity in the majesty of an eternal King. This reverence is not naturally discerned or learned. It's birthed by a personal relationship that forever unveils the mysterious nature of God. Man can only move beyond the introductory echelon of worship when he's progressing down a path not traveled for external blessing but worn by the steps of those who desire to know Jesus.

We live in the presence of God, but we've been called to dwell in His glory. The danger is that many get caught in an emotional struggle concerning the balancing act between fleshly and spiritual desires. We struggle with finding the ultimate will of God. Many have been dissatisfied emotionally and physically because of what's perceived as an inability to find God's perfect will. In efforts to seek the location of His divine destiny, we've grown weary, worried, afraid, stressed, sick, troubled, cold, calloused, depressed, isolated, and confused. These times are dangerous, for it's during these times that the enemy wants us to perceive that we're alone in this struggle.

God's people are often caught in a crunch of a hope that God desires to bless beyond human comprehension. We feel that it cannot be His will to struggle financially, be emotionally devastated, or be afraid and stressed. However, when confronted with the reality that God has an agenda that's greater than blessing, bigger than our bank accounts, and more valuable than our emotional stability, we wrestle within.

God does have an agenda that He's called, saved, and prepared us to engage. This agenda is bigger than all of us, and the enemy knows that if we're sidetracked by personal mishaps, misfortunes, and struggles, we can never fully engage in God's Kingdom.

We live in a world full of crisis, conflict, and chaos. This causes many to live in fear that at any moment calamity could strike, forcing one to face disaster. We're unsettled and unhappy in life, simply because we lack understanding about God's will. His grace is so powerful that He protects through life's darkest places. He empowers us every step of the journey to take the next step. There's nothing we go through that will not bring us to a deeper revelation of Him.

God has prepared promises for us. He must then be allowed to prepare us for those promises. God has designed some of life's greatest difficulties to create a dependency and faith that can only be forged in the fire of affliction. He knows every step of the way. He knows what's needed in every arsenal. He continuously works to bring every saint into fulfillment of purpose. There's no moment outside of

His grasp. There are no surprises. He's aware of every obstacle, barrier, or trap placed in the pathway. He provides invisible evidence during the journey that keeps the weary and wary soldier patiently pounding the earth with his feet, marching until revelation dawns. If we pay close enough attention in the storms of life, we find Jesus walking on the waves, desperately wanting to reveal Himself in the inopportune moments, desiring to make known a power He couldn't demonstrate any other way. Once a person determines that God is working for good, he or she will discover apostolic power.

In his message entitled "Mind the Gap," the well-spoken Christian-apologist Ravi Zacharias told of a prayer that he once prayed and the soft answer that God replied. The prayer and response are powerful.

He prayed, *"Your ways mystify me, Oh Lord. Oh yes, in some journeys I feel You all the way, never doubted. But sometimes You seem to vanish after half way of that journey, and other times you appear to me in the very last moment. And you know, Lord, sometimes I actually fear that You will let me go over the edge."*

He stated that God spoke this reply, *"You are unique my child, and I will help you learn of me with that uniqueness in mind. You see, if I took everybody all the way, Ravi, where is room for their faith? If I took everybody more than half the way, where is room for their love? If I did not let you at times feel abandoned, where is room for My cross. You are not what you will someday be. I am who I am, and I know how to get you from who you are to who I am. If you do not understand this, where is your hope?"*

God has a purpose for your life. However, He also has an

agenda that's even bigger than His will for you personally. He's created your journey to connect with the bigger tapestry of what He's doing in this world. Only by removing perspective from man's limited view and attempting to understand it through the view of eternity, can we truly grasp the magnitude of our importance to His purpose.

His personal plan for a man is always secondary to His Kingdom purpose. That's why true humility is so crucial in the Kingdom of God, because if one lives to make every decision based on what appears best for himself, his family, and his plans, he'll be miserable. One cannot seek God's perfect will without first measuring His Kingdom purpose. Life is not about me. It's all about the Kingdom.

Jesus encouraged believers to cast their cares on His shoulders. He instructed them to understand that His yoke is easy, and His burden is light. To the casual observer the words of Jesus make no sense. How can a yoke be easy? How can a burden be light? The very nature of these two objects determines that they're neither easy nor light. However, Jesus insisted that this were true. Once the onlooker steps closer, he clearly sees what Christ was trying to convey. The reason the yoke is easy and the burden light is because you're not carrying it alone. It's His burden, His yoke. We're merely linking to His plan and purpose. The reason burdens become too great is that we often try to do it our way, which always gets heavy.

We make the will of God too complicated. God's will is first a journey, then a destination. A child of God will never arrive in a final will of God on this earth. There's always more to territory to capture, darkness to illuminate, evil to battle, love to spread, and God to discover. That's why God's will is by nature progressive, for no man can discover all there is of God. He's far too vast and powerful.

The will of God isn't for us to discover all of God. It's merely to become connected to Him in a way that allows continual revelation. When we embrace God to the point that His heartbeat and ours become one, we're ready to be used mightily by His Spirit. When I feel His pain while among the lost, when I feel the warmth of His smile as someone succeeds, when I feel His compassion for the needy, when I feel His heart break as He's rejected; only then am I prepared.

One cannot possess these attributes without a true connection with Jesus Christ. We desperately need that intimacy usher in the divine gifts and anointing of apostolic ministry, for if I love God with all my heart and am connected to Him, my desires will be so interwoven with His that I simply cannot step out of His will. I will not desire anything else.

One of the greatest setbacks that we unknowingly encounter is that we want God's perfect will before we have truly loved Him, and that is disastrous. Many people miss their calling for failure to understand that the call is greater than God's purpose for an individual's life.

The call changes everything, as it prepares one for a commitment to another world. The call reaches beyond you. Therefore, pursuing your calling means responding to a big God in ways that exponentially expand your boundaries. His will is bigger than we can comprehend. We must destroy small thinking. We must break down the barrier of our own worlds and stick our heads out of the sand to view the complete picture.

It is erroneous to teach others to examine their own passions, limitations, and strengths in order to find God's will. Those concepts are a small part of navigating the journey, but we can never discover God's will by looking within ourselves. Ultimately, God's will is not about us. We cannot find the answer through deep contemplation and meditation. It's not about getting in touch with inner emotions. The will of God is about getting in touch with God, and until we have entered an intimate relationship with Him we'll never live inside of His will, regardless of how much we seem to accomplish for His Kingdom. The first responsibility is to a person, not a position or performance. Before we can ever be called to a job or a location, we must first feel and commit to Jesus. If we cannot complete the first step of connecting with Him solely because we love Him, we cannot move forward into the beauty of His Kingdom work. We must connect with Jesus.

The Bible is full of evidence that if men had been given the poor advice to discover their talents and discern their own roles, they would've never completed the work for which they were created. The ultimate will of God is more about listening to God than knowing yourself. No career counselor would've looked at the unimpressive resume of a physically handicapped shepherd and picked him to lead a revolt against the greatest superpower on earth. Few Sunday school teachers would've told an unimpressive, rejected teenager that he would unset the lineage of a king by destroying a trained killer on a battlefield. No corporate headhunter would have recruited a Christian killer to shape the church into an apostolic powerhouse. However, God did, because his will and purpose are bigger than the story of one's personal life. We must engage God first. That's His primary will for everyone.

CONCLUSION: REACTIVE CHRISTIANITY

The devil is thrilled, and God is sick of reactive Christianity. So many Christians live based on what we're against instead of demonstrating WHO we are for. The effectiveness of evangelism is weak when we're known more for what we oppose than the true love and compassion that Christ personified. This isn't to say that outward holiness and all other Christian virtues should be omitted. I'll never join the ranks of those who profess that holiness and Godly living are no longer necessary. On the contrary, in a world of compromise, when people are searching for something real, it's more crucial to live holy than it's ever been.

However, it's a trick of the enemy to convince us to prop ourselves up on Christian laurels. In reality, the love of God walks out on those who do nothing but judge from lofty pedestals. We cannot live with merely a mentality of holiness by subtraction. Under this philosophy, holiness is the byproduct of removing certain elements from one's life. The belief is that if I can get rid of enough carnality, I'll become holy. However, this always fails.

Subtraction is part of holiness. However, man can

subtract everything possible and still be carnal. If he hasn't added a relationship with the Almighty, he is still not holy. Subtraction only hides the filthy rags under pretty clothes of religiosity.

It's possible to do nothing wrong yet be lacking because you've done nothing right. True holiness is about more than running from what is wrong with the world. It's more about connecting with what is right. We cannot become so intoxicated with subtraction that we forget about what we should be adding. One can only become holy by connecting to Jesus.

In the beginning was the Word, and the Word was with God, and the Word was God.

John 1:1

And the Word was made flesh, and dwelt among us, (and we beheld his glory, the glory as of the only begotten of the Father,) full of grace and truth.

John 1:14

The Word or Logos (thought, expression, spoken word, or message) was never fulfilled until it was being lived out. Its fullness wasn't revealed until it had the confines of a fleshly inhabitant. God revealed that His eternal purpose will thrive in temporal vessels. His will is that His eternal purpose be lived out. He desires a voice, hands, and feet. He longs for His love to be displayed. That's what led Paul to discuss to the church at Corinth that they were living epistles. We're the letters written on the tablets of the heart. We're the Word made alive. We have to become the Logos in living, breathing, and working form. We must become the body of Christ, if we're to dwell in apostolic authority.

10
PRISONS WITH STAINED GLASS WINDOWS

There's nothing more stifling to true apostolic ministry than the modern concept of a local church. This concept is far different from the one that thrived in the book of Acts. The early church, founded by Peter and the other disciples, led by prominent ministers such as Paul, and started in a prayer meeting, differs from today's church model in many ways.

Ministry in the early church was undertaken outside of church walls. People came to church and devoted their lives to following the plan of salvation only after their physical needs were met in the streets on which they lived. There was no habit of bringing someone into a church building to meet Jesus. The early church had a clear understanding that Jesus refused to be restricted to a building made by men. They knew that He would forever be found wandering the streets, mingling with the poor and needy, and destroying Satan's strongholds. Jesus refused to be a fixture in a permanent dwelling place. He'd been nailed down only once, and that was to pay the ransom for lost and hurting people. He paid for our salvation and healing, purchasing not only spiritual promise, but also the right to fulfill natural needs. From Golgotha's hill forward, Jesus refused to be forcefully affixed to man's standard. He was ready to take the authority and power He'd paid for and utilize it where it was needed most. Jesus was concerned about building the Kingdom, not building an assembly, and there is an enormous difference.

This chapter is not to argue that the current church structure is wrong. It is to urge Christians that although we are greatly blessed with buildings and central locations, we should never isolate God to only working in the walls of our assemblies. We must become vessel that house apostolic power at all times, even outside the safety of our own congregations.

The early church knew that sometimes people would need to be met and dealt with on their own terms and in their own environments. There was no overriding belief that a person was required to attend service to meet Jesus. In modern Christianity, a person feels threatened before they have a chance to be changed. Some feel that they must meet certain requirements, look a certain way, and attend certain meetings before God will move in their life. This should not be.

God waits on the church to respond to people's needs in

apostolic authority. However, the church waits for the needy to break through their comfort zones and attend our services. Many times, people of other faiths will not attend apostolic churches because they feel threatened. They're being asked to step out in order to receive something from God. In many cases, their own religions (that they are highly devoted to) demand that they not attend services of other denominations. Jesus never required a person to conquer personal fears to meet Him. The early church never stipulated that the sinner pretend to be anything different to find grace or healing. Jesus and the early church met people with no pretences, agendas, or conditions. They just wanted to change lives.

Modern concepts of the church have led to a convoluted system of religious rituals primarily designed to strengthen the body of Christ (which was the main purpose of tabernacles in the New Testament). The early believers attended church to grow in their relationship with God. Most often, contrary to current church philosophy, Biblical church services were more like prayer meetings. Jesus even called the temple a "house of prayer." People weren't afraid to leave the tabernacle and engage their culture when Christ opened the door for Salvation to be spread to the Gentiles.

At the beginning, a few early apostles overzealous to protect Jewish custom, fought against the integration of other people into their way of life. However, as Paul and others worked diligently to spread the message of Christ to all parts of the known world, personal prejudices and fears were surrendered to the greater call of outward evangelism being promoted by the presence of a sovereign God.

Today, prejudice and fear aren't the main culprits keeping

the church from returning to its rightful place as the body of Christ. The cause of today's separation is an earthly mandate that demands obvious lines of demarcation between the world and the church. Lines and boundaries are necessary. Separation from the world is part of the very fiber of the apostolic movement. However, holiness was never intended to lock God into the location of a building or keep believers from stepping into the darkness with the light of God's Word. The current trend is to bring darkness to light, sinners to the saints, and the condemned to the changed. In God's world, the light was always meant to permeate darkness. We were intended to move boldly into the world to make a difference.

Modern church philosophy has become particularly concerned with Satan's alleged attempts to infiltrate the church with lust, selfishness, guilt, pride, and rebellion. Worldliness is creeping into the body of Christ at an alarming rate. Therefore, prevailing methods are inundated with concepts that lock the church into fixed positions, disallowing members to become involved with secular society for fear of losing ground to the enemy. The church has fortified itself against the oncoming onslaught of darkness, taking a defensive posture to rid our hallowed ground of all that's evil and impure. In essence, the church has been designed to keep carnality out.

The foremost problem is that the very people the church has been commissioned to reach are carnal. Without God, all are lost and degenerate sinners. However, they cannot be treated as such. God must be allowed to demonstrate His perfection and power in their lives.

The second principal concern is that we often discover that what we've carefully constructed to keep sin and evil out, also keeps God secluded. We make remarkably little impact on the world, because we attempt to build churches and not the Kingdom. We've created for ourselves, and God, a prison with stained-glass windows. We, much like the Pharisees, have incarcerated Jesus.

The sad, inevitable truth is that while the church burdens itself building fences from the onslaught of sin, the world looks at the church to try and recognize Jesus. This principle is not a new one. People have always looked at His body to view Him. Thomas stated that he wouldn't believe Jesus had risen unless he could touch His scars. The women that came to find Jesus' tomb needed to see His body to judge if He was dead.

Today, nothing has changed. The only evidence the world has that Jesus Christ is alive and well is by looking at His body (the church). The only source the world has to know that He still works is by seeing His hands and feet in action. The only verification people have to know Jesus still saves is by looking at those who have been revolutionized by His powerful presence. The only confirmation those in desperate need of a miracle have that He still performs is by witnessing the testimony of those who've been rescued from a world of hopelessness. The world cannot know the truth about Jesus unless His body restores itself to the prominence and privilege that was intended. The church must open the prison doors and return to the principles that made it powerful in the beginning. We must get back to the roots of being truly apostolic.

THE KEYS

We must return to an apostolic infrastructure that released God's presence and carried Him to people. Freely we have received, and He desires that we freely give. We must become motivated to serve a higher purpose. Every Christian must embrace a personal commitment to a corporate vision for a kingdom purpose.

These are three essential keys to an evangelistic, apostolic revival. A commitment to these three actions will place one directly in the will of God. Anyone desiring apostolic ministry must seek God first according to this plan. The three levels are: developing a personal relationship with God, submitting to the corporate vision of a prayerful man of God, and unselfishly surrendering to a Kingdom purpose.

Every journey toward ministry and true Christianity must begin on the level of a personal commitment toward God. Any step toward this level of devotion must start at the level of humility. True, Christ-like humility has disappeared from the forefront of modern theology. In most cases, the promotion of self is advocated to end the issues of low self-esteem, depression, and anxiety that sweep America. We live under a worldview that promotes self-pleasure, over-indulgence, rewarding of laziness, instant gratification, minimal risks, and "dog eat dog" aggressiveness. "I" is the most distinguished letter in the English Alphabet, because it's the letter upon which most of American life hinges. The crux of American Christianity is not conducive to apostolic ministry. One must live counterculture if true latter-rain anointing is going to be demonstrated.

Jesus taught that humility is vital to the propagation of true anointing and power in His church. It was no accident that God came to the earth the way He did. Jesus clearly defined that humility is not about grand appearances or personal promotion. It's not about inflating one's ego or building one's emotional status. Jesus proclaimed and personified a life that was meek and lowly of spirit. Jesus also demonstrated that humility is about serving others. It's not about doing well. It's about trusting that one's own story is better written with ink from someone else's pen. There's no greater demonstration of humility than when one submits to the will of God without questioning what they'll receive in return.

Jesus went to Calvary at the request of the Father. "Not my will but thy will be done," was His only stipulation. He didn't ask what His reward would be. He was willing to endure the heart-wrenching pain of the cross simply because it was the purpose for which He'd been created. He lived submission and obedience, which is never easy, because they run counter to human nature. However, anointing never flows through a vessel that's not submitted to a man of God. God's Spirit always flows from the top down. If one claims to be anointed, but fails to submit to a man of God, he or she is on dangerous ground. One must then question the validity of the spirit they're entertaining. True submission is an absolute necessity in order to see God's will.

Christ also demonstrated that true humility is not about making one's self look good. He had no form or comeliness. He was not attractive to those around Him. Often, what God calls one to involve in is too risky when first revealed. If one's mission for God feels satisfying to the flesh, most often it's been birthed in the center of one's own psyche. However, true humility ensures that the believer doesn't stray from the path for which he's been chosen, regardless of the risks involved or the lack of apparent benefits along the way.

Jesus displayed that ministry is a collaborative effort. It's about serving the Kingdom of God. Personal recognition fades in the purpose of the Kingdom. Every person chosen by God plays a role in Kingdom development. Humility determines that no role is of lesser value, for worth is not determined by the task being completed, but the purpose for which the task is being undertaken. The Kingdom itself is what gives every duty value, and it is equally important regardless of the job description. Therefore, humility that precedes apostolic ministry views the purpose of the whole, not the effort of the one.

A Kingdom mentality is important in apostolic ministry. Many would argue that the whole is only the sum of the parts. Each part can detract value from the whole. However, in the Kingdom that simply isn't true, because only the Creator determines value. We cannot begin to fathom His purposes.

Some would argue that growing individual churches is what each leader should find most important. After all, the Bible does say, "They added to the church daily." However, once one understands the concept through which the early apostolic movement operated, it's clear that they weren't referring to the importance of growing only the local assembly. They were referring to the church as an entire body, the Kingdom of God. Under this philosophy, saving a soul was most important, as long as they were in the Kingdom. If we could understand, there are no large or small churches in God's eyes. We're all one big family. We're part of the bride, His body in action on this earth for His benefit. We are the Kingdom.

This concept cannot be birthed without effective prayer. People who do not pray are not humble, regardless of their soft-spoken nature and apologetic manner. Prayerlessness is the ultimate demonstration of flesh being in control, regardless of how spiritually inclined one may seem. This is the reason that false humility is so rampant in Christian circles today. Power without prayer is not possible. The Kingdom is still defined, defended, and determined by men and women who submit their flesh to the cross.

Far too many talented, young Christians fail to realize that one can be productive without prayer. One can impress people without prayer. One can impact a church service through emotional performance without prayer. One can even gain influence through charisma without prayer. However, one can never be apostolic in nature without a prayer life that moves Heaven. Jesus was able to tell the world,

"He hath anointed me to preach the gospel to the poor; he hath sent me to heal the brokenhearted, to preach deliverance to the captives, and recovering of sight to the blind, to set at liberty them that are bruised,"

Only because He first stated, "the Spirit of the Lord is upon me."

The second key is to understand the absolute importance of submitting one's own will to a corporate agenda. God's design has always been to flow through a man, speak something into His spirit, and have that anointed vision transferred to others. Solomon, the wisest man outside of Jesus Christ, stated,

"Without a vision, the people perish."

There's nothing that can replace the importance of an anointed man or woman of God. One must have a pastor and other elders who they can be accountable to. Accountability is a concept that's counter to human nature. Man desires to be free of ties that bind or restrict in any way. However, refusal to yield to the authority of an anointed leader is foolish.

Leaders are not only there to protect, but also to ensure that one continues to walk in the anointing. If this principle is ignored, God will never send the anointing. Many young ministers fail because they refuse to submit, arrogantly thinking that because God has gifted them, they're above the ones who have weathered the storms of deception that have already passed. We need the vision and wisdom of the elders to keep us grounded in today's confusing world.

Everyone who truly desires to be apostolic in nature must surrender to the corporate vision of God. Unity is vital to every major apostolic movement that's ever occurred. There's no force more powerful than people of God in agreement. God made the promise that He would show up when two or three people unified for any purpose in His name. A vision always unifies, bringing people together for a common purpose.

The greatest danger to a God inspired vision is the intellect of well meaning but insensitive Christians. Fleshly enlightenment is reserved for Buddhism. One should never be allowed to cast a vision if they're not prayerfully doing so. Flesh isn't able to cast a vision worth pursuing, if the goal is absolute Kingdom effectiveness. A vision born from the flesh tends to promote self. In the end, it's usually divisive, causing more disloyalty than unity. The tendency of casting a vision from flesh is that one gets upset when everyone doesn't choose to follow. However, if the plan is God's, there's no cause for panic or concern. We must be personally committed, and we must have a Kingdom purpose.

The third key is a commitment to a Kingdom purpose. God has always had a purpose for His Kingdom. Before the worlds were formed, there was a Divine destiny in the mind of God. This destiny has never diminished. The purpose of the Kingdom hasn't deviated despite the introduction of man's chaos and self-imposed limitations into God's perfect, ordered universe. Even the rise of false prophets preaching physical prosperity, the accumulation of self-seeking and oversensitive servants, governmental intrusions, religious opposition, demonic assaults, doubting Christians, economic barriers, struggling saints, egotistical and arrogant converts, and weak churches have not been able to slow the fulfillment of His Holy purpose. God's will continues to thrive despite the mind boggling physical, mental, emotional, and spiritual attacks of this detrimental hour.

The purpose of God's Kingdom is to destroy the devil and save the lost. That's the essence of revival and apostolic anointing. When one is devoted to the King, the purpose of the Kingdom is personally revealed, and there's no going back. When one truly loves God, they are consumed with an intimate love for others. These two loves go hand in hand, for one cannot exist without the other. The purpose of the Kingdom is to fulfill the desire of the King, and it is not the Father's will that any should perish. God's greatest desire is for His church to engage in His work. He longs for His body to act in the apostolic nature for which it was created.

THE EARLY CHURCH

One doesn't accidentally become apostolic. It happens on purpose. There must be intent. One doesn't become powerful in God by being reactionary. God is methodical and has a purpose behind every detail that's revealed. That's the reason we must become more than robotic and traditional in methods and meaning. God desires to complete a new work in the church, and that work can never be complete unless the body becomes authentic in who Christ has called it to be.

The sad reality is that one doesn't believe unless true change has occurred. Knowledge without application brings disconnection. The distance between man and God only grows when man learns God's will but fails to apply it on a personal level. We cannot be truly anointed in the dimension God desires for the 21st century church unless we connect to His 21st century purpose. We must stop pretending to be authentic by modeling the religious media moguls who seem to be successful in attracting people. Crowds have never been the defining characteristic of the apostolic movement.

Converts are the result of true power, but conversion to a doctrine born from physical attraction is not the purpose of the cross. The blood forever speaks to change lives.

People are not delivered and set free by happenstance. True deliverance is the result of a surrender that can only occur under the conviction of apostolic anointing. God desires a new work, move, and power to overshadow His people. However, although the work is newer and more powerful, the recipe for revival has not changed. What was born in the Spirit must be re-birthed the same way. We must not deviate from the methods demonstrated by the book of Acts church. Any methodology that dilutes the power of the church compromises God's apostolic agenda. To be truly authentic in apostolic nature, we must ensure that we're pursuing God the way He encouraged the early church to pursue Him.

The early church had remarkably defining characteristics that are easily targeted by the enemy under the pretext of postmodern relativism and political correctness. The unity of the early church is one commodity that has long since been significantly challenged. The ability and responsibility of the church to edify itself has been lost. The nature of humanity is selfish, and the enemy uses every weapon in his hellish arsenal to cause a rift between those in the body of Christ. Most of the problems within the body would never occur if the people involved were prayerfully walking in the Spirit. However, unity is short-lived within most local assemblies, as many church's attempt to keep people together through natural means. The sad reality is that unity will never be achieved through natural programs. True unity will never occur by spending time together, attending the same functions, or sharing the same beliefs.

The early church understood that unity is gained though the mingling of blood, sweat, and tears, as people gather on the battlefield to wage war against the dark tide that's rising against our existence. Once people become engaged in the fact that they've been selected to stand together for a significant purpose, true unity is monumentally recognized. The nature of humanity needs a cause, and there's no cause more powerfully uniting than the call of God to battle evil and change the world.

This uncommon unity shared by the book of Acts church created within each believer an awareness of others before an awareness of self. This outward awareness forged an allegiance throughout the body of believers that caused them to share all things in common. In America, that concept would be considered socialistic. However, the body of Christ didn't share to keep each other fed and clothed. They placed all their valuable possessions on the altars in an effort to reach the world with the message of Jesus. They gave all their natural wealth to make the Kingdom more effective at reaching the world.

I'm not suggesting that one cannot be truly apostolic unless he or she has sold all possessions and given the proceeds to the local assembly. I have enough sense to realize that doctrine would die in today's culture. However, until the body reaches a place that it's willing to give everything if required, it will never realize the full potential of apostolic ministry. Until we become so engrossed in Kingdom living that no personal sacrifice is too high, we are not consumed with Christ to the point of the early church.

The early church was concerned with the spiritual, emotional, and physical well being of sinners. They had an uncompromising attitude toward the influential prince of darkness that could not be negotiated. They recognized that many earthly needs are the result of spiritual disillusionment. Most long-term, negative emotions are directly related to unresolved spiritual issues. I'm not advocating that every struggle a person endures is the result of sin. The Word teaches that it rains on the just and the unjust alike. Life and circumstance happens to us all. However, at times spiritual principle can be violated when no sin has been committed. These violations may not be heaven or hell issues, but they debilitate the quality of life. For example, if one makes undisciplined financial decisions but has not transgressed the Law, he or she is still secure in their salvation. However, that doesn't mean they'll be blessed enough to pay off their debt. At times, wisdom must prevail independent of the issue of sin.

The early church was unrelenting in its approach at reaching the lost. The forerunners of this apostolic experience did not preach the gospel in a spiritual level only. The message was so transformational that it affected every area of their lives. As a result, they couldn't ignore the plights of those around them. They knew they had the power to bring complete deliverance and healing for every physical, mental, and emotional need. It's harder to ignore needs, when one is thoroughly convinced that he or she has the answer. Active faith is revolutionary. It was woven in the very fabric of the first world-shattering church.

The early church challenged every aspect of their political landscape. Governmental pressure and liberal movements that threaten religious groups today would not have created panic in the first apostolic church. The early believers were beaten, stoned, boiled alive, tortured, ridiculed, whipped, thrown in prison, bound in stocks, starved, cast out of society, hanged, trampled, and still held their faith, refusing to allow their voices to be silenced. The liberal agenda would've been afraid to mingle with the apostolic movement of the book of Acts, as the early Christians were unyielding in their response to self-appeasement and self-actualization. Many philosophers have previously stated that the only requirement allowing evil to prevail is the inactivity of the good. It's inexcusable that the majority of Americans still consider themselves to be Christian, yet the majority of outlets influencing the political climate promote only liberal beliefs. The silent majority must live in such a way that their voices are not silenced.

Edmund Burke is quoted:

> *"...duty demands and requires that what is right should not only be made known, but made prevalent; that what is evil should not only be detected, but defeated. When the public man omits to put himself in a situation of doing his duty with effect it is an omission that frustrates the purposes of his trust almost as much as if he had formally betrayed it."*

The church must live to destroy the works of the devil. That's one reason Jesus came to the earth in human form. He wanted to establish His body on the earth through the church. The world is desperately waiting for the manifestation of the sons of God (Romans 8:19). Once God's children are revealed, every domain of influence is challenged. The spiritual atmosphere of the world will change.

The political landscape is merely a reflection of what's taking place in the spirit world, and the enemy is afraid of a church that will arise and counter every despicable and selfish agenda that he's pushing. The church will be fruitful and powerful, only when it has embraced its role to influence every facet of society. We need people to promote God in public forums. We need men and women who will promote God's agenda and declare His righteousness. As long as darkness is the only voice heard, revival will never sweep our communities. However, when the light shines, the darkness is driven back, misleading voices are silenced, and the clarity of God's presence speaks. We are His voice.

. . . . .

The elderly man dejectedly stooped his head in humbled reverence. He'd been praying for hours and had almost been caught up in another world. The experience had only seemed like minutes, but as it started to fade, he was already questioning. Surely God had made a mistake. However, he knew what he'd felt. He knew the voice that had spoken to him. It was the same voice that he'd responded to countless times, and it had never led him wrong. Powerful results had been realized because he'd never questioned. He reluctantly knew that he couldn't start now. He would have to do what the Spirit had asked.

Even as he recognized that fact, he still contemplated talking himself out of it. Maybe he should pray about it more. Maybe he should consult the trusted elders. Thinking of the others worried him. They'd swear he was mad. He'd spoken to many people before and had seen God change their lives immediately, but this task was terrifying. He was being asked to console a killer.

His emotions were mixed at best. On one hand, he realized the value of every soul and knew that to God, even the most despicable characters needed a chance at redemption. On the other hand, he had a difficult time not being judgmental. This man was responsible for murdering people he knew. If he were an attorney, he would've been taken off of the case. If he were being selected for jury duty, he would've been left off of the panel. In either case, they would've ruled a conflict of interest. He was one of the outspoken proponents of the early church, having spoken several times to whoever would listen about the death, burial, resurrection, and ascension of Jesus. The man he was being asked to meet was the biggest murderer of Christians in the known world. He was a spiritual assassin, an apostolic headhunter. Saul was dangerous.

Many of the elders had been praying that God would judge accordingly and remove this threat from the people forever. Ananias pondered all of that for a moment, before finally settling on the notion that God's ways were infinitely more wise than his own. If God saw the value in saving this man, it was because this life was salvageable. The elders and their wives had prayed for God to end the threat by eliminating this man. However, it appeared that God had chosen to remove the threat by recruiting instead of removing. God wanted to turn the Christian killer into an apostolic missionary, and Ananias was right at the center of God's plan. Although his purpose would never match that of the man he was about to reach, Saul would never have embraced the doctrine without the warmth and compassion of this great, yet little known missionary.

Is it not strange how God would smite someone with blindness and speak to him in order to save him? However, countless others have drifted aimlessly along the path of destruction with no supernatural or divine intervention. What made Saul more remarkable than the others? Was his soul of more eternal value? Why would God select him as a candidate for salvation, while allowing others to be lost?

Saul was no more valuable than anyone else along the journey. The answer to why he was chosen creates shock waves that reverberate through the climate of the societal landscape. He was preferred because he was a pawn. He was the perfect weapon in the hands of a God who desired to reach beyond His chosen people and confound a world with the truth of Christian love. God longed to enter a relationship with every man, not just a few. God needed someone who could bridge that gap created by the strong Jewish bias at the time. Paul was the perfect candidate, because he was able to balance both the Jewish and the Roman customs and legal requirements. If properly converted, Paul would be able to lead the charge of getting the gospel through to countless Gentiles. He was a commodity that Jesus used to benefit the Kingdom.

God confronted one man in order to save many. Paul

would become the voice to spread the message that would one day save multitudes. Jesus demonstrated how active He is concerning the principles of His kingdom. He allowed others to drift toward oblivion while forcing one to recognize Him. He was willing to do this, not because of the merits of the one, but because in saving that one, He would be better equipped to save the masses. God has never been afraid to use unfair methods to reach the majority. He'll always do whatever it takes to propagate His message.

The greatest potential for growth of the early Pentecostal church is that they were unashamed to walk in the Spirit. They were Spirit born, and Spirit led. Today's Christian would do well to learn the absolute necessity of walking in the Spirit. The early church seemed to be on location whenever they were needed. The way God used the early apostles to spread the gospel was mind-boggling. God prepared the sinner by dreams, visions, and other thoughts. He'd then send one of his ministers to perform a work. There was no denying that God had orchestrated the event, crossing paths that would have otherwise never merged. This type of ministry is rare in current Christianity. It's become more about mass emails, impersonal fliers, and community events targeting a large number of people together. One-on-one evangelism after being led by the Spirit to minister is atypical. Yet, more will be accomplished by one Spirit led encounter than all the mass-produced promotions that can be generated. If Ananias wouldn't have been following the Spirit, the apostle Paul may not have been saved. However, because one man was sensitive to God, one was saved who would later write over half of the New Testament. How many Pauls are aimlessly coasting through life, waiting on an

Ananias to bring revelatory truth?

The book of Acts church lived, taught, preached, and demonstrated the name of Jesus. No matter what happened, they turned others to Him. They were proponents of the Oneness message, placing the revelation of God's fullness squarely on the shoulders of this Jesus. They taught the message of death, burial, and resurrection as the plan of salvation, equating it to the apostle's doctrine of repentance, water baptism in Jesus name, and being filled with the Holy Ghost. They weren't afraid to use that powerful name. Everywhere they walked, the name changed situations. There was power and healing. Lives were altered. Miracles, signs, and wonders weren't only taught, but also demonstrated as they stretched their faith, all in that name. Demonic strongholds were defeated by the power of that name.

Scripture reveals that demons believe in the fullness of the revelation of Jesus and tremble at the mere suggestion of this idea:

> *Yea, a man may say, Thou hast faith, and I have works: shew me thy faith without thy works, and I will shew thee my faith by my works.*
>
> *Thou believest that there is one God; thou doest well: the devils also believe, and tremble.*
>
> *But wilt thou know, O vain man, that faith without works is dead?*
>
> *James 2:18-20*

Faith and works were both underscored by the revelation

of Jesus on this earth. The one God revelation, which has at its center the absolute truth of Jesus as the only figure in the Godhead, is the precursor to the miraculous. The true supremacy of this doctrine is revealed in the fact that the demonic underworld has this revelation, and the mere suggestion of it strikes fear into their meager existence. Jesus doesn't even have to arrive on scene, just the thought of Him causes the demonic forces to tremble. The demons' faith in God is so strong that it causes a physical response to occur within them. When was the last time your faith was so powerful that it caused a physical difference? There is spiritual dominance that occurs when one knows who Jesus is.

Today, others have placed labels on the apostolic movement in attempts to confine the emphasis placed on the name of Jesus. However, if we are ever to leap back into the powerful display of the gifts of the Spirit that God wants the modern church to emulate, we must do so with a renewed commitment to falling in love with His glorious name. Outside the name of Jesus, we can do nothing. We need that name, not just to open the eternal, but also to weave itself into every Christian's nature. We must re-learn what it means to live as people of the name. That name must be more than a crutch we use to end prayers or solicit the help of Heaven in the midst of trouble. The name must be what we're living for.

The early church was also established on the strong leadership of the five-fold ministry and wasn't ashamed to have the gifts of the Spirit in operation. The modern church desperately needs to embrace the demonstration of the Spirit by supernatural means. Believers must accept the fact that God desires to use them to complete a powerful work in the lives of sinners. He's called all believers to step forward into a reality that demands we be mightily used in the power and demonstration of His presence. We cannot afford to be afraid of operating in the gifts and ministries that God has birthed within us. We must quit being timid about the workings that God is trying to develop.

In current church culture, it's hard to be apostolic. So much importance is placed on natural excellence that many ministers are afraid to attempt the miraculous for fear of failure. Many modern churches stifle the power of the name of Jesus because they're afraid to utilize the gifts of the Spirit in the local assembly. Abuse of gifts has always been a problem. However, the gifts should not be ignored for fear that someone might misuse them. There are many people that God is placing in the atmosphere to birth apostolic ministry.

In discussing this concept with the Apostle Billy Cole, I asked him how a younger minister with an apostolic call gets started on a journey toward the miraculous. I asked how to know when the Holy Ghost was speaking to perform a miraculous work, because at times, I'd wondered if it was just my compassion compelling me to move. His response wasn't what I expected, and certainly made things no easier. Now, it makes perfect sense.

He informed us that the only way to know for sure was to "practice, practice, and practice." He told us that we shouldn't be afraid to fail. Failing is part of the process. It's the only way we could learn to know the voice and will of God. We must learn to trust God enough to quit fearing failure. There's more apostolic anointing waiting to be bequeathed to those who will diligently search. God hasn't finished pouring His power out on this earth, and until He does, He'll always be in need of people humble enough to take the required risk that produces vessels of honor for the Kingdom.

May God supply us all with the audacity to challenge the status quo and delve into the depth of supernatural demonstration through apostolic authority and anointing.

CONCLUSION

If I could summarize the heartbeat of this book in one simple sentence, it would read like this: There is power waiting for every believer who had entered an intimate relationship with Jesus Christ and is fully engaged in His purpose. There is a connection between God's provision and His purpose. We receive power with the infilling of the Holy Ghost. However, that power lies dormant within, until we engage in Heaven's holy agenda, reaching the lost in our world.

The world needs a church to rise from the rubble of rudimentary religion and reach toward a relationship that produces apostolic authority. We're promised authority that supersedes any other era in the history. We've been chosen to make up the church upon which the responsibility for the greatest moves of God, Holy Ghost outpourings, and miracles will come. Many have a passion that propels past ankle deep waters of mundane methodology into the deeper waters of a real relationship with Jesus. Church must become more than an occasional occurrence. Salvation must be more than an initial experience. We must live, breath, and sleep the Kingdom of God. The Kingdom must be operating in our lives at all times. It must become who we are. Luke's words must echo through the corridors of the mind, becoming the quintessence of life,

"For in Him we live, and move, and have our being," (Acts 17:28).

God is creating an army that will manifest itself in a truly apostolic nature and not be confined to modern principles of mainstream culture. The church will once again remove God from the restricting confines of a building, and restore Him to the prominence He enjoyed as the Master of the world. Whenever men and women have embraced Jesus to the point that His heartbeat and compassion for the lost becomes their anthem, true apostolic ministry will be birthed.

We pay honor to all the men and women who bridged the gap between old time apostolic revival and modern evangelical trends. Your sacrifice and commitment to the virtues of the apostolic church will never be forgotten. Let the world rage around us in massive demonic efforts to stop the apostolic anointing and authority that God desires to birth. We will not go silently into the darkness, disappearing into the dullness of disparaging religion. We stand with faces firmly fixed, as men and women of all ages heed the call, lay down their lives, and surrender to the tide of God's overwhelming presence.

ABOUT THE AUTHOR

Jonathan Walton currently lives in Lewisburg, Louisiana. He is a devoted husband, father, minister, author, and leader. He has over 18 years of service and ministry to the Kingdom of God. He has a Master's degree in Audiology from Louisiana Tech University. He loves writing nonfiction books that inspire the believer to move closer to God and challenge believers to reach their world with the message of Jesus. He also enjoys writing fiction Christian books with moral values. His first two books of the B.C. series are now available on Amazon. He is currently in the process of writing his next two fiction books. His desire is to impact lives and challenge the common concepts of today's church in hopes of restoring the Apostolic nature prevalent in the book of Acts.

Dear Reader,

I would like to personally thank you for taking the time to read this book. I hope you were blessed by reading it. I pray that it informative and challenging concerning evangelism. I believe that God will lead and guide everyone who reads these pages into a deeper revelation of His purpose on this earth. If this book has blessed you, please let me know about it. I would be delighted to hear from you. I have also written other fiction and nonfiction Christian books that I'm sure would be a blessing to you. Thanks again for reading.

Forever In His Service,

jonathan r walton

Email me: jonathan@jrwbooks.com

Please learn more at www.jrwbooks.com

For inside information please join my book club at www.jrwbooks.com/insider

Follow me: Twitter @jrwbooks
www.facebook.com/jonathanwaltonauthor
www.goodreads.com/jonathanrwalton

www.ingramcontent.com/pod-product-compliance
Lightning Source LLC
Chambersburg PA
CBHW050630300426
44112CB00012B/1729